Past Forward

T0118310

Past Forward

Essays in Korean History

Kyung Moon Hwang

ANTHEM PRESS

Anthem Press
An imprint of Wimbledon Publishing Company
www.anthempress.com

This edition first published in UK and USA 2019
by ANTHEM PRESS
75–76 Blackfriars Road, London SE1 8HA, UK
or PO Box 9779, London SW19 7ZG, UK
and
244 Madison Ave #116, New York, NY 10016, USA

[© Kyung Moon Hwang 2019]

[The author asserts the moral right to be identified as the author of this work.]

All rights reserved. Without limiting the rights under copyright reserved above,
no part of this publication may be reproduced, stored or introduced into
a retrieval system, or transmitted, in any form or by any means
(electronic, mechanical, photocopying, recording or otherwise),
without the prior written permission of both the copyright
owner and the above publisher of this book.

British Library Cataloguing-in-Publication Data
A catalogue record for this book is available from the British Library.

ISBN-13: 978-1-78308-878-2 (Hbk)
ISBN-10: 1-78308-878-8 (Hbk)

ISBN-13: 978-1-78308-879-9 (Pbk)
ISBN-10: 1-78308-879-6 (Pbk)

This title is also available as an e-book.

CONTENTS

Part IX Trials of Modernization

Part X Gripped by the Past

FIGURES

FOREWORD

How does Korean history connect the past to the present? This question runs through the current collection of short essays, which are adapted from a dedicated newspaper column, "Korean Historical Sense," that I wrote for *The Korea Times* of Seoul from 2014 to 2017.

As a historian I fully recognize the past as valuable in itself, without necessarily a connection to today. But it was not my charge in this column just to illuminate interesting features of Korean history, but rather to consider how history informs a range of current concerns, from national identity to the overlaps between Korea and other cultures. The universalities, then, as well as the particularities of Koreans' historical experience encourage thinking about the impact of the country's past, and especially about the perception of that past, today.

Therefore, a focus on the development of historical understanding, or in other words, on the history of historical views, serves as this book's unifying theme. It seeks to gauge the constant dialogue between Korea's history, from its beginnings to the most recent developments, and Korea's present—an exercise that entails not only considering how the past informs the present, but just as importantly, how the present affects the past. In such a dynamic, then, the present moves backward as much as the past moves forward.

And because this was a newspaper column, I often attempted to let a current concern trigger the historical topic to explore. Some of these original references have been removed in this volume so that it can function as a standalone collection of essays, but it will be clear to the reader that many themes, from politics to culture and international relations, are covered. But all of these essays are undergirded by the core idea that the elasticity of history stretches to transcend barriers in time as well as place.

The essays are divided into ten thematic Parts that all illustrate this general idea. The sections do not appear in any particular order, although the essays within each part are presented somewhat chronologically. Readers who wish to place each essay in the flow of major periods and events are encouraged to consult the chronological and thematic tables of contents at the beginning of the book.

Taken together, the essays forward the following points of emphasis, which amount to a personal ideology of history: First, as a teacher of history I aim to demystify and, if necessary, dismantle history, particularly in regards to the myths and heroes that suffuse every nation's received historical understanding, not just Korea's. In line with this motive, it is important also to shatter romanticized, glorified impressions of the past, such as those associated with and promoted by the royalty, clergy, aristocracy and other dominant elites of yesterday. To paraphrase from one of the essays, the wisdom of the past was not always so wise.

A related point is that, as a historian, I actually wish to de-emphasize history. History is important, of course, but popular or conventional historical understanding is often a product of manipulation, even fabrication, on the part of political and cultural actors. This, too, is not unique to Korea, and the connections in this regard to other countries are very informative. The most egregious examples, though, are arguably from North Korea, and it is critical to understand why and how this state's distorted obsessions with history resulted from Koreans' common concerns and experiences.

To escape the clutch of the past, then, is one of the major challenges and rewards of studying history in the first place. Gaining freedom and relief from recurringly damaging historical patterns and behaviors is crucial, but it is just as important to break away from cherished ways of thinking about the past as an unshakable determinant of the present or the future, whether on a personal, social or national level. This, too, is a universal phenomenon, but in Korea, due to the citizenry's strong historical consciousness, there remains a particularly large potential to fall victim to this process, as well as to gain the rewards of escaping it.

This point was demonstrated well by the developments of 2016 and 2017, highlighted by the demonstrations of millions in the streets, which led to the ouster of South Korea's president, Park Geun-hye, the daughter of a former dictator as well as a representative of powerful interests from South Korea's authoritarian past. That, at least, is how I interpreted the deeper impulses behind those extraordinary events—as ultimately a confrontation between opposing forces and perspectives of history as much as anything else. As the reader of this volume will undoubtedly notice, such circumstances presented an unavoidable, compelling and particularly rich source of understanding for a full range of historical considerations.

It is my hope that the prevalence of such personal perspectives will not appear overwhelming or distracting, and that regardless of where one stands in relation to the author's positions, the reader will find the essays thought-provoking as well as instructive, and hence worthwhile.

CHRONOLOGIES OF KOREAN HISTORY

Political Eras

		Chapters
-4th c.	Earliest Polities	**1, 15, 52, 53**
4–7th c.	Three Kingdoms Era (Goguryeo, Baekje, Silla)	**1, 13, 14, 19, 33, 52**
668–935	Unified Silla Kingdom	**15, 33, 53**
935–1392	Goryeo Dynasty	**1, 18, 19, 30, 52**
1392–1897	Joseon Dynasty	**2, 13, 19, 21, 41, 42, 52, 61, 70, 71, 73**
1897–1910	Great Korean Empire	**8, 26, 28, 45**
1910–1945	Japanese Colonial Rule	**3, 4, 6, 13, 27, 29, 35, 43, 45, 55, 62, 63, 76**
1945–1953	Liberation, Occupation, National Division, Korean War	**1, 29, 34, 52, 59, 60, 62, 63, 66, 72, 74**
1950s–1980s	Early Development of North and South Korea	**5, 13, 29, 50, 51, 56, 61, 63, 64, 66, 72, 73, 74**
1987–Present	Post-Dictatorship South Korea	**6, 10, 50, 51, 67, 69**
1990s-Present	Famine and post-famine North Korea	**32, 47, 55, 60, 72**

Major Events

		Chapters
1st c. BCE	Establishment of Goguryeo kingdom; Chinese Han dynasty commandery in the Pyongyang area	**1, 53**
3rd–4th c. CE	Formation of Silla and Baekje, two of the "Three Kingdoms"	**1, 11, 17, 19**

Date	Event	Pages
6th c.	Absorption of Gaya confederation by Silla	**17**
612	Goguryeo repulsion of Chinese Sui dynasty invasion	**32, 52**
660	Silla conquest of Baekje through alliance with Tang China	**16, 19**
668	Silla's political unification of peninsula through conquest of Goguryeo; beginning of Unified Silla	**1, 13, 16, 19, 33**
678	Silla-Tang War	**32, 52, 53**
890s–910s	Latter Three Kingdoms era of rebellion and fragmentation	**1, 16**
935	Goryeo's reunification of political rule under founder Wang Geon	**1, 13, 16, 19**
958	Implementation of the examination system to select officials	**13, 31**
1000s	Conflicts with various Manchurian polities along northern frontier	**31, 52**
1130s–1140s	Myocheong Rebellion; Compilation of *History of the Three Kingdoms*	**6, 16**
1170	Military takeover of court and government	**13, 71**
1230s	First Mongol invasions; destruction and reconstruction of *Tripitaka Koreana*	**11, 13, 30**
1270s	Goryeo court's submission to Mongol conquest; start of Mongol overlord period; mobilization for two Mongol invasion attempts of Japan	**13, 18, 19, 30, 52, 53**
1350s–1360s	King Gongmin's anti-Mongol actions; beginning of retreat of Mongols	**6, 18, 41**
1392	Establishment of the Joseon dynasty by Yi Seong-gye	**13, 19**
1398	Founder Yi Seong-gye's abdication of the Joseon throne	**55**
1446	Promulgation of the Korean alphabet by King Sejong the Great	**20, 41, 61, 71**
1500s	Literati purges; work of great Neo-Confucian philosophers; onset of hereditary factionalism in central government	**20, 42**

1592–1598	Japanese invasions	**11, 12, 13, 30, 32**
1627–1637	Manchu invasions	**12, 13, 30, 32**
1724–1776	Reign of King Yeongjo	**21, 23, 71**
1762	Killing of Crown Prince Sado	**21, 23**
1776–1800	Reign of King Jeongjo	**13, 21, 23, 43, 44, 71**
1801	First Catholic persecution	**3, 12**
1811–1812	Hong Gyeong-nae Rebellion in northwest	**3, 6**
1862	Major rebellions in the south	**3, 6, 7**
1866	Final Catholic persecution; General Sherman incident; French military incursions	**3, 12, 58**
1876	Treaty of Ganghwa with Japan	
1882	Treaty of Amity and Commerce with the United States; soldiers' uprising; capture of king's father by Chinese	**60**
1884	Gapsin coup; beginning of Chinese protectorate	**45**
1894	Donghak Uprising, Gabo Reforms, Sino-Japanese War in Korea	**3, 9, 10, 25, 26, 28, 45, 65**
1896	End of Gabo Reforms; flight of monarch to Russian legation; start of the Independence Club and *The Independent* newspaper	**8, 16, 45**
1897	Establishment of the Great Korean Empire	**1, 8, 26**
1899	Forced shutdown of *The Independent* newspaper; promulgation of the imperial "State System"; construction of first rail line and the Seoul streetcar system	**26**
1905	Japanese victory in Russo-Japanese War; proclamation of Japanese protectorate	**26, 65**
1907	Forced abdication of Emperor Gojong; establishment of Japanese domination over Korean government	**2**
1909	An Jung-geun's assassination of first Japanese Resident-General Ito Hirobumi	**2, 66**
1910	Annexation of Korea by Japan; initiation of Japanese colonial administration	**1, 2, 26, 33, 43, 65, 66**

1910s	"Military Rule" period; colonial land survey	**13, 26**
1919	March First independence demonstrations; founding in Shanghai of the government in exile, the Republic of Korea	**1, 4, 12, 20, 27, 43, 46, 67**
1920s–1930s	"Cultural Rule" period	**27, 46**
1938–1945	Wartime mobilization during Sino-Japanese and Pacific War; militarized anti-Japanese independence movements	**4, 32, 37, 56, 76**
1945	Liberation from Japanese rule; divided military occupation by Allied forces; violent political contestation in both occupation zones	**34, 35, 62, 72**
1948	Establishment of separate southern (ROK) and northern (DPRK) governments; elections, rebellions and massacres in the south	**34, 35, 59, 60, 62**
1950–1953	The Korean War	**9, 35, 37, 52, 60, 62, 63**

North Korea

Mid-1950s	Purge of potential rivals by Kim Il Sung	**72**
Late 1950s	Cheollima industrialization drive and agricultural collectivization	
1968	Dispatch of commando squadron to Seoul; capture of American ship The Pueblo	
1972	Joint declaration of cooperation with South Korea	
1994	First nuclear crisis; death of Kim Il Sung	**55, 60**
Late 1990s	Severe famine; growth of market activity	
2000	Summit between Kim Jong-il and South Korean president Kim Dae Jung	**47**
2011	Death of Kim Jong-Il; passing of power to son Kim Jong-Un	**72**
2017	Poisoning of Kim Jong-nam, brother of ruler Kim Jong-Un	**72**

South Korea	1960	Student protests over rigged election; overthrow of President Syngman Rhee; establishment of parliamentary democracy	**64, 66, 67**
	1961	*Coup d'etat* led by Park Chung-Hee	**5, 13, 64, 67**
	1964	Student protests over prospective normalization of relations with Japan	**64**
	1965	Signing of normalization treaty with Japan; despatch of troops to Vietnam War	**4, 37, 55, 56, 77**
	Late 1960s	Export-oriented industrialization under Second Five-Year Economic Development Plan; revision of constitution to extend Park's rule	**47, 48**
	1972	Implementation of "Yushin" constitutional dictatorship under Park	**5, 49, 64, 66, 74, 78**
	1974	Opening of first subway line; killing of Park's wife	**6**
	1979	Major protests against Park's rule in southeast; assassination of Park by chief of KCIA	**2, 50, 66**
	1980	Gwangju uprising and massacre; start of military dictatorship under Chun Doo-hwan	**5, 50, 51, 64, 68**
	1987	Mass street demonstrations; establishment of Sixth Republic constitutional democracy; Great Labor Uprising; election of Roh Tae-woo as president	**7, 50, 51, 67, 69**
	1988	Seoul Olympics	
	1992	Election of Kim Young Sam as president	**50**
	1995	Dismantling of former colonial headquarters building	**39**
	1997	Financial crisis; IMF bailout; election of Kim Dae Jung as president	**15, 50, 51, 67**
	2000	Summit between Kim Dae Jung and North Korean leader Kim Jong-Il	**47, 51**
	2002	Co-hosting of World Cup with Japan; election of Roh Moo-hyun as president	**14, 59**

THEMES

	Chapters
Arts and Culture	22, 33, 41, 43, 44, 46, 48, 61
Confucianism	3, 6, 10, 11, 13, 14, 20, 21, 29, 30, 31, 32, 38, 41, 53, 73
Democracy	6, 7, 31, 48, 49, 63, 64, 65, 67, 68, 71, 73
Economy	20, 26, 36, 40, 47, 55, 63, 65, 67, 69, 73, 75
Family and Gender	4, 10, 21, 22, 42, 43, 46, 55, 56
Government	2, 3, 5, 13, 15, 23, 24, 26, 28, 33, 34, 44, 48, 49, 50, 54, 56, 57, 60, 62, 65, 70, 71, 72, 73, 74, 75
Historical Fabrication and Manipulation	32, 53, 54, 57, 58, 60, 71, 72, 74, 76
Holidays and Commemoration	5, 8, 20, 36, 37, 39, 41, 43, 53, 54, 56, 62, 65, 66, 67, 68, 69, 76, 77
Law	9, 10, 29, 74, 75
Media and Popular Culture	18, 21, 23, 42, 43, 59, 61, 68, 69, 78
Military	4, 5, 6, 13, 14, 20, 34, 35, 37, 49, 55, 56, 60, 63, 67, 68, 71, 72, 77
Myths and Legends	8, 16, 20, 22, 32, 33, 41, 53, 54, 60, 70, 71
National Division	33, 34, 35, 40, 44, 47, 48, 49, 60, 62, 63, 65, 72
Nationhood and Nationalism	1, 3, 5, 8, 16, 17, 18, 19, 20, 30, 33, 36, 40, 41, 43, 46, 52, 53, 56, 57, 58, 59, 61, 71, 76, 77
Politics and Ideology	3, 6, 13, 14, 28, 32, 33, 36, 40, 45, 47, 48, 49, 50, 56, 57, 59, 60, 70, 71, 74, 75, 76, 77
Protests and Resistance	5, 7, 27, 40, 45, 47, 48, 49, 56, 57, 64, 66, 67, 68, 69, 74
Regions	3, 14, 15, 16, 19, 47, 51, 68
Religion	3, 6, 8, 11, 12, 33, 38, 70, 71, 78
Social Structure	7, 9, 10, 21, 22, 24, 29, 31, 32, 38, 40, 42, 44, 46, 63, 67, 70, 71, 76

ACKNOWLEDGMENTS

I wish first to acknowledge the assistance and professionalism of Tej P.S. Sood, Abi Pandey, and the rest of the editorial and production team at Anthem Press. I also thank *The Korea Times*, in particular Chang-Sup Lee, Yoon Bae Park, and Young-Jin Oh for their diligence and care and for providing permission to use several of the images in this volume. Finally, many thanks to my family, fellow Asianists at USC and around the world who have offered encouragement, and especially my students at USC who have inspired me to pursue my calling as an educator, broadly conceived.

NOTE ON ROMANIZATION
AND SPELLING

This book uses the Revised Romanization System of Korean, with the exception of certain political figures with well-known spellings otherwise, the city of "Pyongyang," and the surname "Sin," which is rendered as "Shin."

Part I

CIRCULATING HISTORY

Chapter 1

RECYCLING NAMES FOR KOREA

A country's name naturally reflects its history. For example, there are about a half-dozen official monikers for Germany in different regions and languages, a sign of Germany's long and fractured existence before it became a unified state in the nineteenth century.

Korea's story is somewhat different. With the exception of the Mongolian word, "Solongos," which also carries a fascinating history, there are three basic names for Korea around the world: Goryeo (Korea), Joseon and Hanguk. Over its long history, many different expressions have been used, both by neighbors and among Koreans, but these three have become standardized in recent times. Even more interesting is that each of these three terms was revived from an ancient historical period and, in the modern era, underwent further modification in line with political shifts. Such recycling of words for Korea thus shows both the civilization's longevity and its people's awareness of their shared past.

The oldest of the three names is probably "Joseon," which appeared in ancient Chinese records in reference to a political entity on the northern part of the peninsula and extending into Manchuria. This connection later became the basis for national myths about Korea's primordial origins, myths still promoted in both Koreas today.

Joseon was replaced by the kingdom of Goguryeo, a more verifiable state that ruled over the same territory beginning about 2,000 years ago. Contemporary Chinese sources, using colorful descriptions of customs and rituals, described Goguryeo as one of several groups on the peninsula, which included the three "Hans" (Jinhan, Mahan and Byeonhan), tribal confederations on the peninsula's southern half. The term "Han" appears to have come from a native word for "great" or "big," perhaps also "king," but was assigned an ideograph (韓) that referred also to an ancient Chinese kingdom. This added to the confusion, but thereafter the Three Hans, or "Samhan," became a conventional reference for the peninsula.

This was the case even after the ancient Three Kingdoms era (again, confusingly, a term that also referred to a period in Chinese history) came to an end in the seventh century CE with the conquest of Goguryeo and Baekje by Silla. The first reuse of earlier names, however, appeared when this Unified Silla kingdom began to fragment through internal rebellions in the ninth century, as leaders in the northern and southwestern parts of Silla resurrected the names, respectively, of Goguryeo and Baekje. When the leader of this second version of Goguryeo succeeded in militarily reunifying the peninsula in the early tenth century, he stuck with the name, though in shortened form, "Goryeo," as the official title for the new kingdom. This was the word that spread around the world, which explains why outside of East Asia today, variations of "Korea" stand as the uniform term.

During the Goryeo era, however, and even within the country, many other names came into routine use, including "Samhan" (Three Hans), "Dongguk" and "Dongbang" (Eastern Country), "Haedong" (East of the Sea) and "Daedong" (Great East). Most of these terms, tellingly, indicated a strong consciousness of Korea's relationship with China and possibly came from China, but in any case, they functioned as common shorthands among the people.

Such epithets survived even as official, diplomatic designations changed in line with political developments. This happened again in the late fourteenth century, when new rulers brought down the Goryeo dynasty and once more revived an ancient name, this time "Joseon," in order to legitimize the new kingdom's claims over the realm. And such were the motivations when, 500 years later, the formal name again changed, though not in order to signal the death of the five-century-old Joseon dynasty, but rather to give it a new international standing. And in keeping with earlier recycling patterns, the term "Daehan Jeguk", or Great Korean Empire, was established in 1897, although it kept the same monarch, now called an "emperor."

The shortened form of Daehan Jeguk, "Hanguk," thus gained greater use and operated alongside "Joseon," the name ("Chōsen") that the Japanese revived upon colonizing Korea in 1910. The new (old) competing usage did not disappear, however, and Korea's first government-in-exile that gathered in Shanghai in 1919 recycled the "Daehan" and "Hanguk" designations for its formal name, Daehan Minguk (Republic of Korea).

Interestingly, upon liberation in 1945, followed quickly by national division, South Korea used this rendering for its formal name, while the North Koreans kept the name the Japanese had "chosen." North Koreans still refer to their country, and to Korea as a whole, as Joseon, while South Koreans use Hanguk. Their respective names for each other are "South Joseon" and "North Hanguk," which reflects the convoluted history of national division, the ramifications of which naturally extend to naming, including in neighboring lands. In China, they use the preferred terms of the two countries, but in reflecting its longstanding communist alliance with North Korea, the word for Korea as a whole is the "Joseon Peninsula." In Taiwan, they use the South Korean term for North Korea, though interestingly not for South Korea ("South Han"). And perhaps fittingly, the phrasing is oddest in Japan, where it's "North Joseon" (Kita Chōsen) and "Hanguk" (Kankoku), respectively.

All of this recycling and mixing of names may amount to a confusing mess, but even so, it is an intriguing sign and outcome of Korea's compelling historical turns.

Chapter 2

TOPPLING TYRANTS

In mid-2016, at a particularly low point in inter-Korean relations, the new South Korean government of President Moon Jae-in revealed the formation of a special "decapitation" squadron targeting the North Korean leader. Such units had always existed in some form, probably, but the point was to make an impression on such a mercurial, absolutist dictator, as every other approach appeared to have failed.

How to shake some sense into, or better yet, get rid of a tyrant whose behavior seems not just unpredictable or bizarre, but frightening, has been a problem throughout human history. In hindsight, a well-timed assassination at times would have produced an undeniably better outcome. Who could argue against the notion, for example, that killing Adolf Hitler sometime in the 1930s would have prevented much of the carnage around the world in the 1940s?

In Korea's past as well, this challenge arose alongside systematic rules on political legitimacy. Until the twentieth century, as in most other places, sovereignty almost always lay in a hereditary monarch, whose supreme authority came from being the child or relative of the preceding monarch and hence a descendant of the man who originally took power through force. The military leaders who founded the dynastic states, whether it was Goryeo, Joseon or North Korea, established lines of monarchical power in which legitimacy was passed down to the founder's descendants in orderly succession. A new king would formally take the throne once the previous king, usually his father, died.

But this did not always work out as designed. Some monarchs were pushed out by ambitious or merciless royal relatives coveting the throne. Others were forced to abdicate under extraordinary circumstances. The last two Joseon monarchs, Gojong and Sunjong, for example, were stripped of their positions by the conquering Japanese in 1907 and 1910, respectively. And the Joseon founder himself, Taejo, could not stomach the murderous infighting among his children and stepped away from the throne in 1398, just six years after establishing his kingdom.

Throughout the five centuries of the Joseon era, however, only two monarchs were considered so terrible, so dangerous and so immoral that top ministers took the lead in toppling them. The latter of those two, Gwanghaegun, was condemned for his cruelty, although he did not seem any crueler than many other kings. More importantly, he favored making peace with the newly rising Manchus instead of unconditionally supporting the Chinese Ming dynasty in the early seventeenth century, and for that, he was overthrown in 1623.

Recently, however, the historical judgment on Gwanghaegun has undergone a major revision in popular and scholarly circles, and he is now more frequently viewed as a wise pragmatist who foresaw the futility of militarily resisting the Manchus. Indeed, the man who replaced him on the throne, his nephew, had to bow in ritual submission to the Manchu emperor on the outskirts of Seoul in 1637, one of the most humiliating moments in Korean history.

The other deposed Joseon king seems to have been a more clear-cut case. This was Yeonsangun of the late fifteenth to early sixteenth century, whose debauchery and indiscriminate brutality, together with other depraved behavior, present reminders of perhaps the most notorious such monarch in Western history, the Roman emperor Caligula of the first-century CE.

Both Yeonsangun and Caligula were being invoked in 2017 in baffled attempts to characterize the current North Korean leader. Like the other two, Kim Jong-Un had inherited the throne as a young man and seemed extraordinarily unfit to lead, acting capriciously, tempestuously and maliciously on his way toward destroying himself, but not before possibly destroying many other things.

Like the high ministers of the Joseon dynasty wondering what to do with such a menacingly puzzling man, South Korean officials (and perhaps some North Korean ones too) were wringing their hands about the available options and veering toward taking extreme action in their desperation. But we also know that taking this ultimate step likely leads to unpredictable and possibly uncontrollable developments. Furthermore, there is no guarantee that the elimination of Kim Jong-Un would result in a leader who is easier to figure out, although the Kim dynasty itself might cease.

Such lessons also come from Korea's experience with assassinations in the twentieth century, especially the two killings that make up the most extraordinary coincidence in the country's history: the 1909 assassination of the Japanese overlord, Ito Hirobumi, by a Korean resistance fighter; and the 1979 assassination of the South Korean dictator, Park Chung-Hee, ironically by the head of his secret police. The two events took place exactly seventy years apart, both on October 26. It remains curious why the historical reputation of the former assassin, An Jung-geun, is so different from that of the latter, Gim Jae-gyu. Both men claimed righteous justification for killing a ruthless tyrant, but one is considered a national hero and the other a criminal.

More to the point, the results of those assassinations were ambiguous at best. The 1909 killing actually might have accelerated or finalized the Japanese move to colonize Korea the following year, in 1910. And the 1979 shooting led not to democracy in South Korea but rather to a bloody suppression of a mass civil uprising and an even worse dictator the following year, in 1980. History has shown, then, that cutting off the head of a regime does not necessarily destroy the many other actors that serve as its vital organs.

Chapter 3

RELIGION AND SECULARISM

In the historical struggle between religion and government, or "church and state" to use a shorthand, the state has usually taken command in South Korea. This does not mean that a totalitarian state has suppressed all religious activity. Rather, in the name of the public good, political elites have successfully prevented religious movements and institutions from dominating the state.

The result has been a mostly secular state, which has generated a mostly secular public life, even as most people have freely pursued their religious activities. Today in South Korea, for example, one finds a stable coexistence between state and religion, a largely peaceful acknowledgment of shared interests in maintaining separate spheres and religious pluralism. There is perhaps no other major country in the world in which the private religious realm thrives in its diversity, while the public realm remains steadfastly secular.

This reality can be considered a legacy of the Joseon dynasty, when popular devotional practices, such as shamanism or Buddhism, were permitted, just as long as their clergy did not attempt to engage in politics or social movements. When political leaders suspected certain religions of violating this rule, the result was often tragic, as the persecutions of Catholicism in the nineteenth century showed. It was not just the Catholics, however. Throughout the Joseon era, religiously inspired uprisings took place, and the nineteenth century witnessed the three largest such movements, in 1811, 1862 and 1894. The final one, led by followers of the native Donghak religion, almost toppled the Joseon kingdom and certainly helped hasten its end.

Such experiences made state leaders even more wary of religions, especially the often disruptive influence of mass religions like Donghak. When the Japanese conquered Korea and ruled it as a colony beginning in 1910, one of the features of Korean society that concerned them most was religion-inspired social instability. While claiming to permit religious freedom, the colonial regime divided religions into those officially recognized, such as Buddhism or Christianity, and those they called "pseudo-religions." The pseudo-religions, including the many offshoots of Donghak, were potentially dangerous to the political and social order, colonial officials declared. They had good reason to be concerned, as a successor movement to Donghak, together with Protestant Christianity, joined forces to initiate the March First independence demonstrations of 1919.

Thereafter, the colonial authorities kept a careful watch over both Protestantism and the pseudo-religions, as various popular religions occasionally made sensational headlines for scandals or crimes, including nationalist activity. This delicate balancing act came to an end when Korea became mobilized for Japan's total war beginning in the mid-1930s. In the face of protests from some religious leaders, the colonial government pressured Koreans into attending shrine worship observances and erecting altars for Shinto, the native Japanese folk religion, in their workplaces and homes. In time, the colonial state, in effect, functioned as a theocracy. This theocratic order, which worshipped the Japanese emperor, the head priest of Shinto, came closest to establishing a state religion in modern Korea, far surpassing the semireligious role of Confucianism in the Joseon era.

Upon liberation from Japanese rule in 1945, however, a secular state reemerged that superseded religion. In fact, in North Korea, the state came to overwhelm and displace religious life, even as the Kim family itself became the object of religious veneration. In South Korea, the state, after its founding in 1948, never succeeded in imposing itself into the realm of religion. President Syngman Rhee's administration (1948–1960) tried to curry favor with anti-communist Protestant organizations, but this was particular to the circumstances surrounding early South Korea, the Korean War and the intensification of American influence. In general, when occasional attempts, usually led by evangelical Christian leaders, arose to overstep this tacit albeit firm separation between church and state, the public backlash was usually so strong that such efforts were short-lived.

In fact, religions not only prevented state domination in the religious sphere, but even came to challenge the authoritarian state. From the 1960s to the 1980s, the Catholic Church and activist Protestant and Buddhist clergy helped to lead resistance efforts and harbored dissidents of the South Korean military dictatorship. This consistent pressure from the religious realm helped to usher in democratization in the late 1980s, and since then religion has been able to keep in check any interference by state power in religious activity.

But in holding true to the model of a secular society, just as important has been the obverse phenomenon: As in many other settings around the world, the South Korean state, for its part, has mostly limited religion's impact in the public sphere. Therefore, the carefully cultivated principle of religious pluralism has largely escaped being violated or exploited by the interests of any particular religion.

As was the case in the Joseon era and throughout the twentieth century, however, it has been difficult for the secular or semi-secular state to sustain the fine line between the permissible and restricted in terms of religion. Should the state differentiate established, stable, institutionalized religions, for example, from the numerous smaller, popular and unpredictable religious movements? If yes, how so? This remains a major challenge, but one that does not endanger the general pattern of state authority, secularism and pluralism that has developed over the long term in Korean history.

Chapter 4

COMMEMORATING THE
COMFORT WOMEN

The comfort women issue continues to arouse nationalist passions in both South Korea and Japan, as memorial statues are now appearing far beyond the Far East. In South Korea, however, it would be beneficial also to consider the country's own shameful history of sexual exploitation and state-sponsored prostitution.

"Comfort women" or "Comfort Corps" was the euphemism, near the end of Japanese colonial rule, for the military prostitution system servicing the Japanese imperial army in World War II, an offshoot of the "Sacrifice Corps" ("Jeongsindae" in Korean) that produced goods and services for the battle fronts. Various studies over the years have painted a fairly solid picture of how this system worked: The Japanese military helped mobilize and provided the clientele for numerous "comfort stations," run mostly by nonmilitary entrepreneurs (pimps and human traffickers, more or less), that followed the soldiers as they rampaged through Asia.

The question that will never get fully resolved, but which lies at the heart of the continuing controversy, is the extent to which the Japanese wartime government was involved in luring, coercing and brutalizing these girls. This was not a uniform system, and there was a variety of channels that brought the girls to the comfort stations, although most of the victims appear to have been deceived into circumstances that trapped them in the unrelenting horrors of serial sexual servitude. In the end, of course, it does not really matter whether Japanese officials actually managed this system directly, since the Japanese military created and oversaw the demand from its wars of aggression in the first place. The Japanese government, in sum, was responsible for this deplorable reality, and hence this government today should acknowledge and rectify it.

Beyond this general understanding, we would do well to dig deeper into the historical background of the comfort women system and to examine its aftermath. By doing so, we find that the story is more complicated than what is suggested by placing statues in front of Japanese diplomatic compounds or in public parks.

First, as twisted and repulsive as it might seem, the Japanese imperial army's primary interest in cultivating the comfort women system was a military one, that is, to maintain its fighting prowess through a hygienic and "safe" sexual outlet for its soldiers. Raping and pillaging were among this army's primary activities across Asia, and at least the raping had to be controlled and regulated. The Japanese had begun focusing on disease prevention as a most important factor in military success as early as the wars of imperialism against China and Russia at the turn of the twentieth century. And the systematic provision of "clean" prostitution, an extension of the system that had developed over centuries at home in Japan, became an overriding concern.

Here is where Korea comes in. Not only did these Japanese wars take place mostly in Korea, but the resulting Japanese colonial rule, beginning in 1910, drew from these battlefield experiences as well as from the longstanding culture of state-sponsored prostitution and sexual exploitation in Korea itself. We speak here of the nationwide network of "gisaeng" courtesans who functioned, effectively, as government employees in the preceding Joseon era. This was only the most visible feature of the larger culture that connected political and social status with sexual exploitation. In the Japanese colonial period, both these practices and the *gisaeng* were recycled, re-systematized and combined with Japanese traditions to produce a state-regulated prostitution system. The comfort women setup thus built on the foundation of such structures of sexual exploitation that had long developed in Korea.

More evidence that the comfort women ordeals were not only a Japanese phenomenon came after the Japanese rulers retreated from Korea in 1945. The "comfort women" label was retained and became the basis of the military prostitution system servicing the American military in South Korea, beginning around the time of the Korean War (1950–1953). Thereafter, with the unofficial backing of successive South Korean governments, the "camp towns" surrounding American military bases funneled thousands of Korean women into prostitution. The history of the comfort women cannot be divorced, in other words, from the succession of military or militarized dictatorships on the peninsula for most of the twentieth century, beginning with the Japanese takeover in 1905.

Given this, one becomes even more suspicious of the motivations behind the late-December 2015 agreement between the South Korean and Japanese governments. President Park Geun-hye tried to complete this deal within the 50th anniversary year of her father's 1965 normalization treaty with Japan, to be sure. But one wonders to what extent she also sought to whitewash this long history of systematic prostitution supplied to the American military by past South Korean regimes, especially her father's. In any case, South Koreans

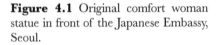

Figure 4.1 Original comfort woman statue in front of the Japanese Embassy, Seoul.

Figure 4.2 Replica comfort woman statue in front of the former Japanese consulate building, Mokpo, South Korea.

driven by understandable anger at the Japanese government would do well to look inward for the causes and outcomes of the comfort women tragedy. Statues are fine, but they should memorialize something more than just Japanese offenses.

Chapter 5

MAY 16 AND MAY 18

Most South Koreans associate the month of May with the many commemorative holidays—for children (May 5), parents (May 8), teachers (May 15) and the birth of Buddha. For historians and many others, however, mid-May sparks commemoration of two signature moments of the recent past.

The first is May 16, or "5–16" as it is known. On May 16, 1961, General Park Chung-Hee overthrew the beleaguered, democratic government and installed himself as the head of a military junta that ran the country until he was narrowly elected as a civilian president two years later. Park would win two more presidential elections, then rule through a constitutional dictatorship from 1972 until he was assassinated in late 1979. Over the nearly two decades in which he commanded the state and economy, South Korea went from being one of the world's poorest countries to one of its most dynamically industrializing ones. Park's assassination, however, resulted not in democracy but rather in another military coup at the hands of General Chun Doo-hwan, who instigated the other major event of mid-May that is annually memorialized: 5–18.

May 18, 1980 was the date, following the imposition of martial law around the country, when protesting students in the southwestern city of Gwangju were savagely attacked by South Korean troops. This triggered a wave of violence that, over ten days, resulted in the killing of hundreds and the maiming of many more. There is little doubt that the Gwangju Uprising (or "5–18") spawned the growing resistance in the 1980s against the military dictatorship and then the mass protests of 1987 that established the electoral democracy of the Sixth Republic, the governing system we still have today.

The historical significance both of 5–18, which later gained formal recognition as the "Gwangju Democratization Movement," and of 5–16 has been subject to heated debate that reflects deep fissures in South Korean society. Needless to say, the controversy surrounding the 2013–2017 presidency of Park Chung-Hee's daughter, Park Geun-hye, only intensified this discord. In fact, supporters of the latter President Park felt emboldened to cast more doubt on the hallowed standing of 5–18, thinking that this would help their efforts to revitalize the positive historical assessment of 5–16.

Some mythmaking about 5–18 did indeed take place. Those Gwangju residents who risked their lives and went into the streets were expressing their outrage and demanding recognition of their human dignity in the face of brutality. They probably were too preoccupied to consider their resistance as part of a heroic narrative of Korean democracy. But as it turned out, official memory turned this into a reality, to the chagrin (still today) of those who condemned Gwangju as a leftist rebellion. When 5–18 came to be viewed as just as significant as 5–16 in the annals of South Korean history, the two events became linked.

It does not take a genius, much less a historian, to draw the connections: One of the sources of 5–18 was 5–16. This is because neither the Gwangju Uprising nor its bloody suppression would probably have been possible, or necessary, without the groundwork laid two decades earlier through the 5–16 *coup d'etat*, called the "5–16 Revolution" by supporters then and now. But one can go even further. If we consider the leadership that ordered the merciless attacks on the Gwangju citizens as the primary culprits of 5–18, then its brutality constituted a crushing of not military or government rivals, but rather of civil society. In this sense, 5–18 completed a short-term process that had begun in December 1979. Indeed, as its perpetrator, Chun Doo-hwan, more or less (and proudly) acknowledged, the model for his December 1979 *coup* was very much 5–16. Therefore, 5–18 could be considered a product of 5–16 in more ways than one.

This realization can prompt a lot of counterfactual scenarios, which as historians we are not supposed to engage in, since we are trained to study what happened, not what might have happened. But such a mental exercise is often irresistible, and in this case poignantly unsettling: If 5–16 had not taken place, would something like 5–18 have happened anyway? And if 5–16 had spawned a mass demonstration (and violent government response) like 5–18, would things have turned out differently for South Korea? Could a durable electoral democracy, for example, have emerged a generation earlier, in the 1960s?

Many say "no"—that South Koreans were not ready for true electoral democracy in the 1960s, and that they needed first a strong, autocratic government to lead them out of poverty and protect them from North Korea. They also insist that only through the defense measures and economic development secured by the quarter century of military rule did South Koreans reach a stage in which they could handle democracy properly. To others, such an argument sounds like a convenient explanation and justification for the way things turned out.

Chapter 6

TRAGEDY AND FARCE

One of Karl Marx's most famous observations was that history tends to repeat itself, first as a tragedy, then as a farce. It is difficult to discern, however, whether the 2016 crisis surrounding President Park Geun-hye and her longtime confidant Choe Sun-sil, which led to the jailing of both, was more of a tragedy or a farce.

The farce was that, once again, we had a major scandal involving bribery and influence-peddling by people close to the president during the closing stages of her term. This had become predictable almost to the point of absurdity. Indeed, in an age of relentless social media, mere hints of dubious behavior led to wild speculation that Park, immersed in a cult founded by Choe's deceased father, turned to Choe to act as a kind of shaman sorceress in making presidential decisions. This notion was patently ludicrous, but the fact that such an idea gained traction was telling, as it pointed to another repeating pattern in Korean history, one with much deeper origins.

Since the ancient era, a tension between "high" and "low" religion has periodically arisen in the Korean political realm. Early Buddhist clerics skillfully absorbed the underlying shamanistic character of popular devotion in order to spread their teachings and gain access to political power, and monarchs in turn relied on Buddhist scholars and monks for advice, spiritual comfort and legitimacy. But Buddhist clerics who could channel personal charisma or popular followings for political purposes also represented a looming danger. Occasionally, a monk gained tremendous influence over political rulers, resulting in crises and even emergencies. In the Goryeo era, for example, the monk Myocheong appeared to hold King Injong under a spell before instigating a major rebellion, and later the monk Shin Don gained such sway over King Gongmin that Shin effectively controlled the court.

The Confucian scholar–officials who founded and maintained the succeeding Joseon kingdom were determined to eliminate this religious influence over state affairs. They tried to preserve a strong separation between what they considered the realm of rational politics and that of popular religion, namely Buddhism and shamanism. They dismantled Buddhist temples in urban centers and even banned Buddhist clerics from the capital. For the most part, despite the idiosyncrasies of individual monarchs, the Joseon dynasty succeeded in limiting such religious influence. In the nineteenth century, however, two of the three enormous rebellions (1811, 1862, and 1894) that shook the country were inspired by popular religions. Even the uprising of 1862, not directly instigated by religious fervor, led quickly to the government's execution of a budding spiritual leader, the founder of the Donghak movement.

When Donghak followers, three decades later in 1894, drove the largest revolt in Joseon history, it seemed to validate the elites' long-standing fear of popular religions. Indeed, the Korean government, even while loosening the prohibitions against Buddhism, restricted the work of shamans and other similar figures. When the Japanese took over in 1910, the colonial regime further systematized this approach by suppressing smaller religious groups and movements on fears that, like Donghak, they could lead to social and political instability.

South Koreans today seem largely to maintain this view that a modern political order should be not duly influenced by popular religious practitioners, especially those who draw on primal behaviors. But there is nothing illegal or even particularly wrong with a president practicing her personal religious beliefs, whether in the form of institutionalized religion or shamanism. Shamanistic ceremonies appear regularly in public rituals, in fact, as they are seen as representative of core Korean traditions. So the widespread condemnation of Park Geun-hye's supposedly superstitious turn to a shaman or cult was itself somewhat farcical. Furthermore, it hid the more sincerely tragic elements of this scandal, which revolved around the central problem with her standing and authority: The support for her was always based on her ancestry, not her personal qualifications. She was, in some ways, a victim of this tragically repetitive historical farce.

Park Geun-hye was raised in sheltered surroundings as the daughter of the ruling president, and in her young adulthood, she experienced the assassination of both her mother (1974) and her father (1979). Could we really have expected anything resembling a realistic perspective on society by someone with such a background? It would have been more surprising if she had *not* been exploited eventually by shady people who provided her comfort and easy explanations for her ordeals.

And yet, none of these considerations prevented hordes of political opportunists and millions of elderly supporters from elevating Park toward the presidency over the preceding two decades, based solely on her parentage. This was a farce from the start: Park's return to public life began when she won an election in the late 1990s as assemblywoman for a district in Daegu, her father's regional power base. Granted, she was born in Daegu, but she had spent almost all her life in Seoul. That this and other absurdities seem not to have mattered forced the country to face, once again, the long-term consequences of South Korea's dictatorial past.

Chapter 7

GENERATIONAL RENEWAL

The mega rallies throughout the country in late 2016 reached a scale unmatched since the mass uprisings of three decades earlier, in 1987, that finally overthrew the South Korean dictatorship. As the democratic system instituted that year entered a period of great turmoil in 2016, and as developments around the world showed a resurgence of authoritarianism, we were reminded of the fragility of democracy, of the need for vigilance, and of the power of mass action against unjust rule.

I would argue, however, that the institutional and public response to President Park's abuse of her office, especially the candlelight vigils that eventually brought down her administration, also provided reassurances of the maturation and sturdiness of South Korea's democratic culture. South Koreans were justified in lamenting their incapacity, it seemed, to escape deeply ingrained habits of corruption, but they did not capitulate to history; rather, they viewed their history, especially the recent past, as a source of encouragement, inspiration, and determination to emerge from this trial with an even firmer democratic foundation.

The strongest support for this optimism came not necessarily from the scale of the demonstrations, but from the faces of the demonstrators themselves, or more precisely their ages: All generations, including children and teenagers, were represented in these peaceful gatherings. Parents brought their kids to the candlelight vigils to show them how to exercise their civic freedoms and responsibilities, and middle and high school students took it upon themselves to voice their concerns.

In this regard, especially striking were the comparisons to the mass protests of the 1960s to the 1980s, including the largest ones ever in 1987. The breakthrough to democracy that year drew on support from middle-aged, middle-class citizens, many of whom were former activists, but overwhelmingly the demonstrators continued to be mostly university students, along with laborers. High schoolers were frankly too busy trying to survive the college entrance exam system that consumed their lives. They had to wait until entering college, when the pressures for academic performance would be greatly reduced, to engage in politics. Indeed the sudden freedoms they experienced, once liberated from cramming, probably contributed to the energy of their extracurricular activities.

Despite the many setbacks, including the implementation and redoubling of military dictatorship in the 1970s and 1980s, these students' cumulative efforts to resist the authoritarian system had an extraordinary long-term impact. They not only resulted in the formal breakthrough to a democratic system in 1987 but implanted in society an increasingly robust culture of democracy. And once they became teachers, workers, professionals, state officials and parents, the former student protestors instilled in the younger generations the core values of freedom, accountability, equal opportunity and social justice.

This transformation did not proceed smoothly, of course, as broader economic forces and other structural factors maintained and even magnified unjust social inequalities. Despite increasing transparency and accountability since democratization, then, the Park Geun-hye scandal of 2016 showed how unfair privileges continued to tear at the social fabric. I am convinced that the remarkable plunge in support for Park that year, including even from her ideological allies, came substantially from revelations of how her friend Choe Sun-sil circumvented or bulldozed the rules governing fairness in educational access. Even conservative parents were appalled at the degree to which Choe's daughter could flaunt her myriad privileges to "attend" both high school and college without actually attending them. This crossed a clear line, if nothing else about this sordid affair could bridge the political divides.

Such behavior surely brought painful reminders of the bad old days of the undemocratic past, when abuse and corruption were rampant, but the positive features, especially the committed struggle to defeat this system, also shrone through powerfully. The continuing development of this democratic culture and the strengthening of democratic institutions laid the groundwork for the 2016–2017 government investigations of bribery and other illegal activities in the realms of education and culture. And most remarkably, prosecutors at various levels summoned for questioning a range of powerful people, including even the sitting president.

None of this would have been possible in the dictatorship period, and surely no one back then could have even imagined prosecutors publicly naming the president an accomplice to extortion and other crimes. This shows that the system of checks and balances worked, and for this, South Koreans who took to the streets in late 2016 were transmitting the legacy of pro-democracy activism from their recent history. Indeed, these protestors fought for the rights of even the counterdemonstrators, consisting overwhelmingly of senior citizens, who acted reflexively to protect their cherished impressions of a simpler past.

But unlike them, those acculturated in the generational renewal of democ-racy took the 2016 crisis as an opportunity to further strengthen the republic. As in 1987, the successful overcoming of the emergency might even eventually lead South Koreans to consider more fundamental reforms, perhaps even to institute a parliamentary system of government. This might be the best way to ensure that South Korea can continue as a thriving democracy just as other places in the world waver from this path.

Part II

DURABLE TRADITIONS

Chapter 8

MARKING THE NEW YEAR

In ancient times, civilizations around the world figured out the basics of the earth's relationship to the sun and the moon, and from this, they learned to count the days, months and years. But other factors also played a role, including political and religious power, and hence most methods of marking the New Year actually have not corresponded to scientific principles.

One of the exceptions is the Persian New Year (Nowruz), which comes on March 20, the date of the vernal equinox. This is when the sun's most direct rays cross the equator along the earth's northward tilt, and hence it technically marks the beginning of spring (or the fall, in the southern hemisphere).

Koreans traditionally recognized the vernal equinox as well, as the start of one of 24 seasonal periods (*jeolgi*). But this did not signal the New Year, which was set by a calendar that combined measurements of both the moon and the sun. What is normally called the Lunar New Year (*Seollal*), the country's most important holiday, is based on a complicated system that counts a year as having passed through 12 of the moon's 29- to 30-day cycles. But as with other traditional holidays based on the lunar calendar (such as Buddha's Birthday or the Chuseok harvest festival), the date differs slightly every year, because 12 moon cycles fall several days short of the 365.25 days that it takes for the earth to revolve once around the sun.

In sum, because Koreans customarily have used multiple methods to mark the passage of time, the New Year has a complicated history. More than a century after the formal adoption of the Gregorian, or "Western" (solar) calendar, in fact, there remain two distinct New Year's Days in Korea, with January 1st being in many ways less important. The first new New Year, on January 1, 1896, came somewhat suddenly in the middle of the 11th month of the lunar year equivalent to 1895. This was decreed as part of the revolutionary changes implemented by the Gabo Reforms, which began in the summer of 1894 and ironically ended soon after the inauguration of the new solar year of 1896.

The government's adoption of the Gregorian calendar would survive, however, as would the observance of a New Year and dating system adopted from a civilization and religion, Christianity, that most Koreans at the time did not know. But such were the pressures to integrate global standards in the era of Western imperialism.

However, Korean calendrical systems had long contained political elements. Official documents before the modern era, for example, were sometimes imprinted with the year of a particular king's reign (e.g., the "10th year of King so-and-so's reign"). Or more often, the name of a year was determined by the Chinese calendar, which in turn reflected the emperor and dynasty ruling China at any given time. In 1894, the Gabo Reforms put an end to this practice, which had signaled Korea's political and cultural subservience, by counting the years in reference to the native Joseon dynasty. That year, for example, was the 503rd year since the "Opening of the Country," or "Gaeguk 503." The current North Korean system does something similar by counting the years since 1912, the birth year of Kim Il-Sung, the country's founding ruler. 2018, for example, was officially "Juche 107."

The government's adoption of the Gregorian solar calendar in 1896 did not necessarily simplify things. It also did not lead to official use of the numbering system for that new calendar. As Koreans had done occasionally throughout their history, starting in the ancient Silla period, the official calendar marked an auspicious reign name for a certain monarch. For example, 1896 was proclaimed the opening year of the reign titled, appropriately, the "establishment of the solar [calendar]," or *Geonyang*. In everyday life, however, years continued to be counted according to an ancient system, the sexagenary cycle of sixty years that remains in use even today.

Thereafter, political changes added further complications to the counting of the years. Even as the Christian dates became more commonly accepted in practice, the official renderings would change again in 1897, 1907, and 1910, when the Japanese system of referring to their own monarch's reign became implemented in Korea. However, such nationalized dating methods were not abandoned following liberation from Japanese colonial rule in 1945. Until the early 1960s, the numbering of years in South Korea referenced the legendary birth of Dangun, the mythical founder of Korea. For example, 1960 was the year "Dangi 4293."

One might consider this absurd and needlessly complicated. But many, if not most, people in the world today juggle more than one calendrical system simultaneously. Elements of Japanese society, including its government and right-wing nationalists, for example, stick to their emperor-based year names, long after having adopted January 1 as the official New Year. Given this, that Koreans celebrate New Year's Day twice every year seems somewhat tame in comparison.

Chapter 9

SLAVERY, BONDAGE, AND SOCIAL HIERARCHY

In the early 2010s, Americans commemorated the 150th anniversary of their Civil War (1861–1865), which was about many things but mostly became a conflict over the issue of slavery. As the war came to a close, an amendment abolishing slavery was added to the US Constitution, a document that, since the founding of the country, had recognized and even promoted slavery. In the decades preceding the war, however, slavery and the bitter disputes over its place in American society had eaten away at the nation's soul and raised basic questions about its identity and character.

The United States was not the only country with slavery, of course, and various forms of customary or legalized human bondage were common around the world. Koreans themselves long practiced their own brand of slavery, within a population with no physical differences, while that of the United States was based on, and had a lot to do with furthering, the notion of race. But the two slave systems also shared fundamental features, including hereditary slave status and the treatment of slaves as property to be bought, sold and bequeathed. And in both cases, the social segregation of slaves was maintained by the "one drop of blood" principle, which came in response to widespread "mixing" through sexual exploitation. The children of these master-slave unions almost never took the father's social status, and so their subjugated, stigmatized identity was passed down to their descendants.

Furthermore, most people did not question basic notions behind a social order that perpetuated slavery. In the United States before its Civil War, in both the North and the South, almost all White people, whether or not they thought slavery was just, believed in the inherent inferiority of Black people. In premodern Korea as well, the common perspective, especially by those, like slave owners, who benefited from the system, saw slavery as simply the extension of dividing society according to birth. And as with the United States, Korean society came to depend economically on this organized means of human exploitation.

In both societies, however, there also emerged scholars, clerics, officials and others who vehemently condemned slavery on moral and other grounds. And although, unlike in the United States, we have little trace of the voices of the Korean slaves (*nobi*) themselves, there is plentiful documentary evidence of the demeaning, dehumanizing and often brutal effects of slavery.

It was not until the Gabo Reforms of 1894 that slavery was officially prohibited through a simple yet powerful declaration: "Laws allowing public and private public slavery are completely abolished, and the sale of human beings is forbidden." As it turned out, though, this actually did not constitute a sudden or complete change. In the latter part of the Joseon era, political, cultural and economic forces brought forth incremental improvements, including the elimination of government slaves in the early nineteenth century. The proclaimed emancipation of all slaves in 1894, then, was largely a symbolic gesture, and it furthermore did not result in the immediate eradication of personal bondage; indeed, especially in the countryside, servile laborers (*meoseum*) continued to tend to their masters until the middle of the twentieth century.

These legal steps of the late nineteenth century, however, were still significant. Once slavery, bound servitude, and the designation of "mean" or "low-born" people (*cheonmin*) were eliminated from Korean society, the descendants of slaves enjoyed true social liberation. Because Korean slavery, though meticulously maintained through record-keeping and other factors, had not depended on physical differences, the increasing urbanization and mobility of the modern era made it very difficult to determine who had slave ancestry. This stood in strong contrast with the United States, where the racial basis for social discrimination remained important for more than a century after formal emancipation.

Koreans, however, were not easily able to escape their own painful traditions of social bondage and discrimination. The lingering power of social status in determining interpersonal relations and access to resources took different forms in the early twentieth century, but it probably accounted for the tremendous appeal of communism and other utopian ideals. In this sense, the nation's own civil war, the Korean War of 1950–1953, had more in common with its American counterpart than what appears on the surface.

In South Korea, the effort to overcome the long legacy of inequality developed into a growing and fierce insistence on social justice. Combined with other ideologies such as nationalism and democracy, this ideal helped sustain the people's resistance to dictatorship and to the concentration of economic power. Still, the opposite tendency also persisted, as some privileged Koreans mistook their inherited economic or social advantages as expressions of some natural or proper order, and they perceived and treated their less privileged countrymen accordingly. As in the United States, the conflict between these two opposing forces, which in many ways continues a longer struggle to account for the legacies of slavery, remains central to the drive to forge a better society.

Chapter 10

MARRIAGE, ADULTERY, AND CONCUBINAGE

In February 2015, South Korea's Constitutional Court issued a ruling that decriminalized adultery. Although rarely enforced or enforceable, there had been a law, passed just after the Korean War in 1953, that sentenced anyone found guilty of extramarital sexual relations to up to two years in jail. In its 2015 judgment, the court declared that such a law violated an individual's personal freedom, but not surprisingly there arose opposition from various interest groups that decried the potential harm to family life.

What became somewhat lost in the public debate, however, was the law's original intent, which was less about restricting liberties and more about enforcing greater gender equality. In fact, the larger motive was to overcome an institution hundreds, if not thousands, of years old: concubinage. For this historian of Korea, concubinage remains one of Korea's most interesting and long-standing historical problems. I would suggest, in fact, that most of the efforts to reform Korean family practices over the past century or so, including through legislation, have been related to the ingrained practices of concubinage.

Of course, Korea was hardly unique. Concubinage, the institutionalization of extramarital sexual relations between a privileged male and a subservient female, has been a universal phenomenon throughout world history. But the particular turns that this issue took in Korea illustrate some distinctive features of the country's history.

It is difficult to say when concubinage became such a normal aspect of Korean life, at least among the elites, but it probably dates back at least a thousand years, if not more. Indeed, so fixed was concubinage in Korean society that even the fervor of (Neo-)Confucianism, the comprehensive ideology behind the establishment and maintenance of the Joseon dynasty (1392–1897), could not weaken it. Like religio-ethical systems elsewhere after the ancient era, Confucianism appeared to favor the sanctity of marriage as central to the family system. In the early Joseon period, this meant that a privileged Korean man could no longer have more than one wife.

Instead, a woman who used to be considered a second or third wife became downgraded into the status of a concubine, and a concubine's children, who might be raised in their father's household, suffered legal and social discrimination. Indeed, for most of the Joseon era, not only the concubine's children but their descendants, in perpetuity, were forbidden from taking the state civil service exam, which was a marker for a much broader social stigma.

Given the prevalence of concubinage, simple math shows that, after several generations, the population of these concubines' descendants would multiply exponentially. This is exactly what happened, and by the eighteenth century, these suffering people began to organize themselves to seek social liberation. They achieved some measurable successes, but no fundamental change could take place while concubinage—which was based on and fortified a wider web of social and sexual exploitation, including slavery—continued.

The Korean officials who forged the Gabo Reforms in 1894 began the modern effort to tackle this problem through legal changes. Not surprisingly, many of these reformers were the descendants of concubines. They focused on the ravages of the traditional family system as a whole, including arranged and early marriage, in order to realize their ideals of modern society. But they, too, were limited in what they could do, for concubinage remained firmly intact.

The Japanese colonial rulers, beginning in 1910, also did little to restrain this practice, and indeed they tread very carefully when it came to changing family customs, preferring a gradual process of displacing the patrilineal Korean family system with the patriarchal Japanese one. The colonial regime thus encountered countless headaches in trying to adjudicate family disputes over inheritance, adoption and divorce arising from concubinage.

Thus, in 1953, the South Korean government took the desperate legislative step of criminalizing adultery to begin to address directly the mismatch between concubinage and modernity. The complex issues of sexual freedom, exploitation and gender hierarchy had to be simplified into this admittedly extreme, but understandable, solution, given the equally complex and long history of this matter in Korea.

Chapter 11

BUDDHISM AND KOREAN IDENTITY

Figure 11.1 Jogyesa Temple in downtown Seoul.

Buddhism remains perhaps the cultural form most closely associated with Korea as a distinct civilization. Just as European countries can be viewed as products of a "Judeo-Christian" tradition, East Asia can be seen as "Buddhist-Confucian." It has been said that, regardless of their formal religious identities, all Koreans (and perhaps all East Asians) are, at heart, Confucians. But it would be more accurate to state that all Koreans, whether they recognize this or not, are Buddhists.

Figure 11.2 Bulguksa Temple, Gyeongju, South Korea.

The ties between Buddhism and Korea run so deep that Buddhism even preceded the formation of a coherent country on the peninsula and helped shape Korea into its early forms. Traditionally Buddhism has been traced back to the fourth century, when it was introduced from China, and thereafter it played an indispensable role in the political and cultural formation of the Three Kingdoms of Goguryeo, Baekje and Silla. The close relationship between institutionalized religion and statecraft, which would characterize Korean historical development for more than 1,500 years, began in this ancient era, as Buddhist clerics helped advise and provide legitimacy to political leaders.

As a religious entity as well, early Buddhism established abiding patterns in Korean civilization. The first of these was ecumenism, or the harmonization of religious diversity. Instead of excluding or repressing the indigenous folk religions on the peninsula, Buddhist leaders absorbed and even celebrated them. This approach, as part of Buddhism's core teachings of finding spiritual relief from the hardships of human existence, provided a durable connection to the populace and sustained the general approach of inclusivity up to the modern era. Embracing native religious forms in the early years also established Buddhism's close connection to Korea's environment and geography, as temples and rituals absorbed the shamanistic worship of spirits and deities attached to nature. The primacy of the terrain in Korean identity was

Figure 11.3 Wooden Blocks of the *Tripitaka Koreana*, Haeinsa Temple, South Korea.

further developed by Buddhist clerics who adapted the ideas of geomancy to conceive of the peninsula as a living being fed and shaped by its countless mountains and rivers.

At its peak in influence, Buddhism also inspired and promoted some of the greatest achievements in Korean art and architecture. But perhaps most impressive was the Buddhist clergy's extraordinary advances in printing technology. Today some of the oldest examples of woodblock printing in the world date to the Silla kingdom of the eighth century, with the high point reached in the mammoth project, accomplished twice no less, of constructing printing blocks for the entire Buddhist canon, or *Tripitaka*, during the succeeding Goryeo era. When the first set was destroyed by Mongol invaders in the thirteenth century, a second set was carved into more than 80,000 wooden blocks, which remain housed in Haeinsa Temple, near Daegu, today.

Not surprisingly, Buddhism was also responsible for what is often deemed Koreans' most impressive technological invention, movable metal type printing, which took place two centuries before Johannes Gutenberg's machine of the fifteenth century. And not surprisingly, the oldest extant book in the world printed with movable metal type is a Korean Buddhist work, recently repatriated to South Korea after more than a century of being held in France.

This brings us to another component of Korean identity for which Buddhism played a key role: perseverance and growth. Just as the Buddhist clergy undertook the *Tripitika* project as a means of helping the nation survive foreign attacks threatening to decimate Korean civilization itself, throughout its history, Buddhism has had to adapt and struggle to survive. The first such crisis began in the late Goryeo era, when its long preeminence in the political realm appears to have resulted in decay and corruption, which rendered the Buddhist order a ready target for Confucian reformers. When these Confucians established the new dynastic rule of Joseon, the Buddhist clergy were stripped of their political and economic power and forced to retreat, to the private devotional realm in their social influence and physically away from the cities. But this they did, perhaps taking advantage of becoming freed from political entanglements to focus on providing spiritual solace to the people. All the while, Buddhist clerics retained their role as protectors of the nation, contributing manpower to repelling the Japanese invasions of the late sixteenth century, for example.

The most recent challenge to Korean Buddhism's viability and strength came in the early twentieth century. In the face of Japanese imperialism, on the one side, and the less domineering but equally provocative influence of Christianity, on the other, Buddhist leaders had to adapt to the new notions of "religion" as something bound by fixed rules, expectations, and relationships to both state and society. Despite these and even more menacing threats, especially from fundamentalist Christians, in the latter twentieth century up to the present day, Buddhism has persevered through constant adjustment and rebirth, reflecting its core teachings and outlook.

In South Korea today it is difficult to escape the enveloping "ethos" and sentiment of Buddhism, especially in the arts such as literature and film. Whether they identify themselves as Buddhist or not, the creators of these cultural products are paying homage to the undeniable centrality of Buddhism in Korea's cultural identity, a product of nearly two millennia of history.

Chapter 12

CHRISTIANITY'S RAPID RISE

Outside of the Philippines and enclaves such as Armenia and Georgia, South Korea remains the only country in Asia, home to more than half of the world's people, where Christians make up a substantial portion of the population. In historical terms, this means also that Korea became perhaps the only civilization where Christianity grew into a major religion without the aid of colonial or political domination. But in some ways, its development and ultimate acceptance repeated, in abbreviated form, the difficulties that the religion suffered initially in southern Europe and the Levant nearly 2,000 years ago.

There were probably some people in ancient Korea, beginning in the Silla kingdom of the fourth to tenth centuries, who had heard of Christianity through traders. But this did not lead to any lasting community of Korean Christians, and the religion did not draw any significant attention until the sixteenth century. That was when Jesuit priests made their way to China and Japan, where they worked as scholars and teachers and even attracted some converts. One convert, in fact, was a general who helped lead the Japanese invasion of Korea in the 1590s. (His new Catholic faith apparently did not deter him from ordering the mass slaughter of innocents.)

After the Manchus subdued Korea in the 1630s on their way toward conquering China, they took a Korean prince as hostage, and it was whispered that, while in captivity in Beijing, this young man took an interest in Catholicism. However, those Catholic priests in China were very limited in their influence because they could not readily leave the capital city and were not allowed to proselytize openly.

It took another 150 years for the first Korean Catholic, Yi Seung-hun, to appear. Yi, part of a diplomatic mission to China, became baptized in Beijing in 1784, after which Chinese priests and their Korean sympathizers began secretly to evangelize within the peninsula. There, the Confucian elite became very concerned, because it appeared that Catholicism promoted the abandonment of well-established notions of social order and ritual behavior. When King Jeongjo, who had called for a "wait-and-see" approach to Catholicism, died in 1800, there followed a severe persecution of Catholic converts in which hundreds, perhaps thousands, were killed. For the early Korean Catholics, the first two-thirds of the nineteenth century represented a brutal period of trial and constant danger, not unlike the first three centuries of Christianity under the Roman Empire. The thousands of Catholic martyrs were later sanctified as having made the ultimate sacrifice for the faith.

About a hundred years after Yi's baptism, Christianity gained formal recognition in Korea amid the country's "opening" to the outside world in the late nineteenth century. Protestants from the West, as diplomats, educators and physicians, carried an aura of progress and advancement, which helped Christians in general, including Catholics, to gain a legal foothold on the peninsula. This process, however, also spawned severe tensions and confrontations.

Once into the early twentieth century, in fact, the political impact of Christianity, particularly Protestantism, was just as important to its growth as its association with Western advances in medicine and education. At the same time as the Japanese takeover of Korea, a revivalist form of Protestant Christianity, influenced by American missionaries, took hold, especially in the northwest. In the early part of the Japanese colonial period, this Protestant community, led by foreign missionaries and Korean clergymen, maintained an uneasy coexistence with the colonial regime. Such tensions were shown most starkly in the Protestant leaders' central role in the March First independence demonstrations of 1919.

Many of these figures eventually worked out a functioning compromise with the colonial government, but some did not. When the authorities demanded that students in Christian schools participate in rituals to honor the Japanese emperor, some Protestant leaders chose to shut down their schools rather than engage in what they considered sacrilegious behavior. This persistent Protestant resistance to the Japanese might have heightened the faith's appeal among Koreans, who embraced it in increasingly greater numbers.

Following liberation in 1945, the next major chapter in Christianity's political role began as the Soviet army occupied the northwestern region, the center of Korean Protestantism. This led to the persecution and the mass flight of Christians in the years leading up to the Korean War of 1950–1953. After the war, these northern Christians' bitter memories of their experiences fueled their ideological support for anti-communism, driven by dictatorships, as a dominant feature of South Korean society. The cultural and political influence of former northern Koreans in the shaping of South Korea remains an extremely important, complex topic to be further explored, but undoubtedly the religious impact was among the most important.

Not all Christians were so fervently anti-communist and pro-regime in South Korea, however. The Catholic Church, in particular, became a staunch advocate for democratization, social justice and human rights. In the 1970s and 1980s, the leaders of both major Christian branches, including some Protestants originating from the north such as Ham Seok-heon, published anti-regime books and journals, harbored dissidents, and organized resistance efforts against the South Korean dictatorships. For today's Christians, this can be considered one of several proud legacies of their faith's fascinating history in Korea.

Chapter 13

CIVIL–MILITARY BALANCE IN POLITICS

A durable tradition in Korean history has been the balance between civilian and military control over politics, a dynamic that remains somewhat fluid today. As elsewhere, most major shifts in governing form, from the establishment of new kingdoms and dynasties to foreign conquests, came through military means and were led by military men. Through the influence of Confucianism, however, in Korea an overriding principle of civilian control over the military, instead of the other way around, emerged relatively early.

In the ancient era, the recurring rivalry among the so-called Three Kingdoms from the fourth to seventh centuries was followed by Silla's conquest, with military help from China, of the other two kingdoms. Two centuries after the beginning of this Unified Silla kingdom, however, local strongmen emerged to challenge its rule, marking a period of internal conflict that lasted several decades until coming to an end through the exploits of Wang Geon, a local military leader from present-day Gaeseong. In establishing the Goryeo dynasty, Wang reunified the Silla territory, incorporated new lands in the northern part of the peninsula, and consolidated his control through strategic marriage alliances with dozens of other local strongmen.

However, Wang's immediate successors to the throne prevented a military domination of politics by implementing a Confucian governing system, including state examinations for selecting officials. Eventually, though, this civil supremacy, for complex reasons, induced a backlash among military officials, who overthrew the civilian government in the late twelfth century. Thereafter the peninsula came under the hereditary control of military officials, who nevertheless maintained the sovereignty of the Goryeo kings. Ironically, not long after taking over, these military elites themselves came under the siege of the Mongols, who would eventually conquer and rule Korea, Manchuria, China and much of Eurasia over the next 150 years. Like the Korean military elites before them, however, once the Mongols secured control over the peninsula, they allowed a civil-dominated governing form to take hold.

As the Mongolian overlord period came to an end in the latter fourteenth century, another Korean military figure emerged, Yi Seong-gye, whose ancestors had served the Mongols in the northern fringes of the Goryeo realm. Like Wang Geon, though, Yi shed his military garb and established a dynastic rule, the Joseon kingdom, directed by Confucian principles of civilian command. Unlike Goryeo, however, the Joseon dynasty successfully cemented this hierarchy between civilian and military, and such an orientation prevailed in not only politics but the rest of society as well. It helped that there were no major external threats in the first two centuries of the Joseon era, but even after the devastating Japanese and Manchu invasions of the late sixteenth and early seventeenth centuries, the military never came to dominate Korean life.

So this relationship between civil and military rule followed a somewhat repeating pattern since the Silla unification of 668: long stretches of peace or internal stability, followed by bursts of major political or dynastic change driven by military action that, in turn, established a firmer foundation of civilian rule. Such a cycle took another turn in the late nineteenth century with the onslaught of imperialism, which toppled almost permanently the long-standing general hierarchy between civilian and military forms of governance in Korea.

The Japanese had perhaps the most to do with this. Japan gained control of Korea through two major wars at the turn of the twentieth century and colonized the peninsula with a heavily militaristic approach. Not only was the colonial government, which began in 1910, led always by a Japanese military commander, but the legions of soldiers and military policemen spread a way of life that elevated the martial. This became even more the case when Korea became mobilized for total war in service to the Japanese empire's aggressive expansion in the 1930s and 1940s.

As it turned out, Japan's defeat in World War II and Korea's liberation in 1945 did little to return the peninsula to a subordinated standing for the military. The circumstances of the postliberation period, framed by the American and Soviet superpower occupations, only increased the standing of military solutions and military figures. In North Korea, a former anti-Japanese communist guerrilla fighter, Kim Il-Sung, took control and promptly launched the Korean War in 1950. Thereafter, North Korea became perhaps the most heavily militarized society in the world, as the entire population became permanently mobilized for war in order to maintain the totalitarian rule of Kim and his descendants.

In South Korea, a heavily anti-communist state ideology, intensified by the Korean War, laid the foundation for its own military strongmen to appear. This happened first with the *coup d'etat* led by Park Chung-Hee in 1961, and for three decades thereafter regimentation and political violence pervaded

South Korean life. The onset of democratization since the late 1980s has witnessed a return to civilian control over the military, the culture of which has gradually retreated to the barracks. As long as the North–South confrontation of national division remains in place, however, the return of militarization remains a possibility, however faint.

Chapter 14

REGIONALISM IN ELECTIONS

Upon first glance, the map of the April 2016 general election results for the National Assembly looked similar to immediately preceding ones, in which the contiguous territory of the conservative party's geographical strongholds looked like the vowel "eo" in the Korean alphabet. The other two blocks represented, respectively, the capital region and the Jeolla provinces (colloquially known as Honam), which previously often showed a common preference, but not this time.

Indeed upon closer inspection, the election map suggested that familiar regional patterns were starting to break down, especially in the major cities. Of course in industrialized democracies often the most important factor in elections is the economy, particularly the employment market, the price of everyday goods and other pocketbook issues. And the 2016 election suggested that the chronic financial insecurity of younger citizens pushed them to the polls to voice their displeasure with the ruling party. Furthermore, one is inclined to believe that the 2014 Sewol ferry tragedy, the second anniversary of which approached during the election campaign, framed the political perspective of many grieving citizens. Still, South Korean electoral behavior continued to reflect ingrained regional identities formed over decades, if not centuries or even millennia.

While it is tempting to consider rivalries that originated as far back as the Three Kingdoms era of 1,500 years ago, which the electoral maps somewhat resemble, the more reliable historical connections are to recent periods. We can begin with the Gyeongsang provinces, or Yeongnam, the former territory of ancient Silla but more importantly the long-standing bastion of Confucian orthodoxy, even when this fierce identity sometimes deprived this region of national political power in the Joseon era (1392–1897). These residents' conservative inclinations also led to a slower embrace of modern change in the late nineteenth and early twentieth centuries, which matched well the anticommunist, authoritarian streak of the military figures from Yeongnam who ruled South Korea from the 1960s to the 1980s. These dictatorships established a corridor of industrial development connecting Gyeongsang to the capital region while largely excluding the Jeolla provinces, or Honam. And the political, bureaucratic and economic favoritism enjoyed by Yeongnam cemented its ideological leanings, as seen in electoral behavior that defied the liberalizing impact of democratization.

Furthermore, so dominant did Yeongnam become in national politics that, with one exception (the late President Kim Dae Jung), every single president over the past half-century, both before and after democratization, has come from this region in one way or another. And this includes not only staunch conservatives but even the most liberal presidents, Roh Moo-hyun and Moon Jae-in, who both hailed from Busan. But this also points to a major difference between North and South Gyeongsang province. Northern Gyeongsang, home of the military dictators and the geographical base of the main conservative parties, has remained doggedly traditionalist and slow to change. Southern Gyeongsang, though, while still generally conservative, has had a very different history, one of democratic resistance and labor activism under authoritarianism. And the results of more recent elections show that, as a political region, southern Yeongnam continues to diverge significantly from its northern counterpart.

Opposition to and victimization from dictatorship, as well as the championing of democracy, have determined more firmly the political orientation of the Honam region in the southwest. A hotbed of resistance to economic concentration and exploitation dating back to the Japanese colonial period of the early twentieth century, the Jeolla provinces suffered greatly from the inequalities of South Korea's emergence thereafter. Not surprisingly, this region has proudly identified itself as the cradle of Korean democracy and social justice, an identity consistently demonstrated in past elections. The 2016 general election results, though, showed a remarkable shift.

Whereas, in the past, Honam voters had reliably backed the main "progressive" or "democratic" party, this time they voted almost as a solid block for a new third party, the People's Party, led by someone from Busan. Jeolla voters have supported figures from southern Gyeongsang before, such as Presidents Kim Young Sam (eventually) and Roh Moo-hyun, as well as the latter's protege Moon Jae-in. Much more than the regional background of the candidates, then, a refusal to support the conservative party associated with the past dictatorships has proven decisive.

It appears that this principle has been less influential in the Chungcheong provinces, which came close to splitting their vote between the two main parties. Compared to Jeolla or Gyeongsang, historically Chungcheong has experienced greater difficulties in maintaining a secure regional identity, as if it were stuck between the surrounding regions and unsure of its standing. Chungcheong voters have therefore tended to remain loyal to major personalities from their home region, although in reflecting the legacy of the Joseon era, when this province boasted a concentration of hereditary elites (the "yangban"), these figures have tended to be conservative.

Such a legacy has had a different impact, however, on the capital region, Gyeonggi, and on Seoul, the grandest stage for political contestation and, in South Korean electoral history, the bellwether for the nation as a whole. This has been particularly true because the capital area, without a deeply rooted regional identity, steadily became a destination for people from all over the country as it underwent rapid urbanization and industrialization.

The 2016 parliamentary election, in which the capital region's citizens voted overwhelmingly for the main opposition Democratic Party of Korea, thus likely reflected the continuing hold of such transplanted identities, at least to some extent. In any case, the election results pointed to a further weakening of traditional regional voting patterns shaped so powerfully by history.

Chapter 15

YEONGNAM'S STRONG PRESIDENTIAL POLITICS

Despite the major shifts in regional electoral patterns suggested by the 2016 parliamentary elections, in terms of presidential politics, as shown a year later, things had not changed much at all. The candidates from the four main parties in that presidential election of spring 2017 all hailed from the same region: Yeongnam, or the Gyeongsang provinces.

Granted, the two from southern Gyeongsang, centered in Busan, were further left of center ideologically than the two from northern Gyeongsang, centered in Daegu. This bifurcation continued historical patterns, however, as the two previous presidents from Busan, Kim Young Sam and Roh Moo-hyun, were both on the "liberal" side of the political spectrum. Likewise, the five previous presidents from northern Gyeongsang, including the deposed Park Geun-hye, were undoubtedly "conservative."

Such a history takes us to the larger issue of how and why Yeongnam has dominated presidential politics, if not quite South Korean politics as a whole, for nearly the country's entire existence. Since the 1960 popular overthrow of the first president, Syngman Rhee, whose roots were in Hwanghae province of northwestern Korea, nearly every president with real authority (thus, not counting Yun Boseon and Choe Gyuha) has come from the Gyeongsang provinces. The single exception was Kim Dae Jung, from neighboring and rival Honam, or the Jeolla provinces, and he barely won amid an economic crisis in 1997, after having lost three previous presidential elections to Yeongnam candidates. In sum, it has been very hard for someone outside Yeongnam to become president.

Equally remarkable is the fact that none of these presidents, dating back to the founding of South Korea in 1948, has come from Seoul. (Park Geun-hye came closest, as she had spent almost her entire life in the capital, but her familial ties to her birthplace of Daegu were more important to her electoral success.) The rapid urbanization over the past half-century, which produced the megalopolis surrounding the capital, drew migrants from across the country, and therefore the local identity of the capital's citizens seems to have remained weaker than the ties to their original home regions.

This explanation is not incorrect, but a fuller answer, based on a more thorough analysis of historical evidence and data, is likely a lot more complicated. The same holds true for Yeongnam's dominance, but we can begin exploring this issue by turning to some broader verifiable patterns in modern Korean history. First is the fact that Yeongnam has long enjoyed a population advantage. Although the capital region contains nearly half of the country's people today, the Gyeongsang provinces have a lot more than the other regions, with about a quarter of South Korea's population, compared to about 10 percent for Honam.

Actually this relative strength in numbers has decreased over the years. According to the South Korean government's online statistical portal, in 1970, Yeongnam had an even greater percentage of the country's population of 30 million, exceeding that of the capital region. Going further back, to 1955, one finds that Yeongnam, which held around one-third of the country's counted population of nearly 11 million, dwarfed that of the Seoul area, which was smaller than even Honam.

The concentration of people in Busan, which during the Korean War served as South Korea's capital and a destination for refugees, explains some of this. The parents of President Moon Jae-in, the candidate elected in 2017, were among these wartime newcomers to Busan, for example. For others, Busan functioned as a dynamic regional capital that pulled in people from surrounding areas. This seems to have been the case for 2017 presidential candidate Ahn Cheol-su.

Busan grew rapidly also due to its Japanese connections during the preceding colonial period of 1910–1945. Located closest to Japan, this port city became the gateway for Japanese domination and for those in the southern part of the peninsula wanting access to Japan. This resulted in Busan's suddenly overtaking the traditional capital of Yeongnam, Daegu, within a couple of decades in the early twentieth century.

But for the Yeongnam region as a whole, the population advantage was grounded further back in history. Published official statistics from 1907 show that the two Gyeongsang provinces, having been recently divided for administrative purposes in 1896, were by far the largest in the entire peninsula, not just the southern half. And the numbers from the 1930 census show that Yeongnam, with just over 20 percent of the peninsula's population, remained the largest region, followed by Honam.

Thus, the Gyeongsang provinces' relative population growth thereafter in a divided Korea, together perhaps with Honam's relative decline, explains some of Yeongnam's domination of South Korean presidential politics. Although this is just a fraction of the larger story, it is worth considering, at least for now, in accounting for the persistence of this regional imbalance.

Part III

ANCIENT REMAINS

Chapter 16

THE BEGINNINGS OF KOREAN HISTORY

In January 1896, the Korean government skipped over the final months of 1895 in order to adopt the Western solar calendar. It even took a new reign name for the monarchy, *Geonyang* ("Establishing the solar [calendar]"), to mark this occasion, as if to signal the rebirth of the country in the modern world. But when was Korea really born? In other words, when did Korean history begin?

As South Koreans continue to wrestle with competing interpretations of their history, it seems a good time to consider this basic question, even though it actually receives little attention. Perhaps this is because most Koreans do not believe there is any question about Korea's origins, or because of the opposite, that this issue is too contentious and controversial. But it is indeed worth exploring because it makes us think about how to conceive of "Korean history" itself. So below are some candidate dates for the beginning of Korean history, as well as the pros and cons regarding their historical validity:

2333 BCE. The fallback, conventional date, when the mythical founder of the Korean people, Dangun, was said to have been born on Mount Baekdu to establish the ancient kingdom of Joseon.

Pro: It is a good story that emphasizes Koreans' common ancestry, an ancestry with ties to the heavens and dating back nearly 4,500 years, which makes it easy to just round up Korea's age to a convenient 5,000 years. With no evidence, the tale leaves little room for countering claims.

Con: There is no evidence. This story first appears in a book of supernatural tales from the thirteenth century, 3,500 years after the supposed event. It is also a bit embarrassing that any nation would consider this kind of account as anything but a fairy tale.

37 BCE. This was when the Goguryeo kingdom, one of the earliest polities on the peninsula with support from actual historical records, supposedly began through the birth of its founder, Jumong, who is said to have emerged from an egg.

Pro: Goguryeo is a good candidate for status as the originating state in the territory that became Korea, since the earliest Chinese accounts of various "barbarians" on the peninsula specifically describe Goguryeo as one of the most impressive (and colorful) groups. Even its name gave birth to the word "Korea," which is how the country became known outside of East Asia. Furthermore, the story of the Goguryeo founder's birth, like that of the founder of Silla, attests to the significance of shamanism, the underlying folk religion on the peninsula, in ancient Korea.

Con: The earliest written evidence for this date comes from the fifth century CE, and even here it is retold as a legend. The remaining support for this date is a listing of the early Goguryeo kings found in the "History of the Three Kingdoms," a book from the twelfth century. This work, however, also claims that Silla's founding predates Goguryeo's by two decades. Not surprisingly, this chronicle is usually seen as having a pro-Silla bias.

668. The year of Silla's military conquest of Goguryeo, which followed its conquest of Baekje in 660 and unified the "Three Kingdoms" under Silla rule.

Pro: This event put an end to centuries of periodic warfare between the kingdoms on the peninsula. Through state administration, it also initiated the social and cultural integration of the people into an identity that eventually came to be recognized as "Korean." There is also plentiful documentation attesting to the details of this process and of this era, beyond royal genealogies.

Con: Silla relied on assistance from China's Tang Dynasty to achieve its military victories over Baekje and Goguryeo. To many Koreans in the modern era, such a move betrayed the nation and established the pattern of cultural and political subservience to China that would continue until the twentieth century. Another objection is that the ensuing reign of "Unified Silla" only controlled about half of the peninsula. The rest became the territory of the overlooked Balhae kingdom, which can be considered a Korean entity since its ruling elite came mostly from Goguryeo.

935. The year of Silla's surrender to Wang Geon, the founder of the new Goryeo dynasty who reunified the peninsula following decades of fragmentation at the end of the Silla era.

Pro: Supported by plentiful historical evidence, there is no doubt that the founding of Goryeo extended the preceding Silla territory northward in implanting a dynastic reign that would last nearly five centuries. Wang Geon and his immediate successors to the throne also further systematized and integrated their political control over the peninsula, and they issued pronouncements about the kingdom's distinctive characteristics and values.

Con: There remain few sources showing that the majority of the people held the same collective identity as that of the kingdom's monarchy and elites. There is little evidence, in other words, that most people felt that they were somehow "Korean" instead of just peasants or slaves who served the upper classes.

This would remain the case until the middle of the succeeding Joseon dynasty, which began in 1392 and, one might suggest, ended in 1896, the year of the calendrical change. To further highlight this sense of renewal, the following year in 1897, the country's name was officially changed to Daehan Jeguk ("Great Korean Empire"), which was shortened to "Hanguk," the same term today for South Korea.

Chapter 17

ANCIENT AND PRESENT GAYA

Some controversy arose when President Moon Jae-in, soon after taking office in May 2017, publicly encouraged greater study of the ancient civilization of Gaya and nominated a particular National Assemblyman for a cabinet position. President Moon vowed to do things differently from his disgraced predecessor, but both of these steps seem mostly to have continued a disturbing pattern.

That pattern has been government intervention in historical scholarship, or more generally the politicization of history. State sponsorship of historical study is not always a bad thing: When, in the previous decade, the South Korean government established a commission to document the hidden atrocities of the Korean War, for example, it overturned a long-standing cover-up from the dictatorship period. Several years earlier, another government decision, to let competing private publishers write history textbooks instead of authorizing only a single official version, had further enhanced the spirit of openness following democratization in 1987.

This explains why the interventions of the preceding president, Park Geun-hye (2013–2016), were so distressing. First, she tried to renationalize high school history textbooks, over the outcry from almost all professional historians, in a transparent effort to resuscitate the historical reputation of her father, Park Chung-Hee, the former president and dictator. This was one of several moves by her administration, including the rushed agreement in 2015 with the Japanese government regarding the comfort women issue, that aimed to break down what was considered a domineering leftist historical orthodoxy.

Regardless of whether historical understanding is dominated by progressives, however, both left and right views, at least among the general public, are undeniably nationalistic. Politicians and other non-historians readily turn to ethnic appeals over history, especially in order to mobilize supporters for historical claims against Japan or China. Thus, President Moon's appointment of Do Jong-hwan as his Minister of Culture, Sports, and Tourism, was troubling. As a legislator, Mr. Do fought against the renationalization of textbooks, but he also called for rejecting major research projects that he deemed insufficiently one-sided, as if somehow he, once a famed poet, knew better than groups of trained historians. And throughout, his intervention came in defense of nationalist fantasies about ancient history that betrayed not only ignorance but an appeal, once again, to tribalism.

Speaking of tribes, that is what Gaya was, a confederation of tribes, and probably little more than that, at least in terms of political character or identity. It was neither "Korean" nor "Japanese," as it was absorbed by neighboring Silla before there was a Korea or Japan. So to engage in this back-and-forth with Japanese historical distortions from the early twentieth century, which by now are nothing more than a convenient bogeyman, is frankly silly. But equally absurd is the widespread acceptance of the legend, spread by the South Korean education system including even universities, that Korean history originated nearly 5,000 years ago, and through a supernatural event at that. The Japanese and Chinese have promoted similar national myths. The claim that Gaya was actually the ancient Japanese colony of Mimana, for example, sought to legitimate Japan's colonial rule over Korea in the early twentieth century.

And so it is easy to see how this situation can produce ongoing tensions over who, in terms of the modern nation-states of Korea or Japan or China, ruled whom and controlled which territory thousands of years ago. This sensitivity flared up again in mid-2017 when apparently the Chinese president told his dim American counterpart that Korea was once a part of China.

One wonders when this will stop. Even opinion pages for sensible press outlets like *The Korea Times* have promoted this nationalistic fervor, accusing Mr. Do's critics of being "pro-Japanese." More sober observers, including professional historians, had hoped that the new South Korean president would be more reasonably dispassionate. But Moon seems to have escalated the situation. And it is not as if there is a lack of scholarly or popular interest in Gaya already. There is in fact a major Gaya museum in Goryeong, a university museum in Daegu, and a national museum and Gaya Theme Park in Gimhae, the supposed capital of historical Gaya. Gimhae, though, is also the hometown of the late president Roh Moo-hyun, a close friend of President Moon, who is from neighboring Busan. So despite Moon's publicly avowed intent of only encouraging more research and attention for the sake of greater harmony between provincial regions, this seemed more like a political move, sadly.

Furthermore, given that the historical figure most attached to Gaya, General Gim Yusin, played the leading role in Silla's conquest of other kingdoms on the peninsula back in the seventh century, the glorification of Gaya has the potential of actually worsening regional rivalries. Such unintended consequences are always a danger when politicians and government officials try to politicize historical understanding. If Koreans can use Gaya to make a territorial claim

Figure 17.1 Entrance to the Gaya Theme Park, Gimhae, South Korea.

based in the ancient era, for example, they should be prepared to countenance Chinese claims over the Pyongyang area.

The other major problem is that such politicization of history tends to ignore or manipulate the work of trained professionals. It thus constitutes a disregard for verifiable facts and trained expertise in order to pursue tribal politics, a component of the runaway nationalism that we see around the world today.

Chapter 18

EMPRESS GI

As a fan of lavish recreations of historical settings in TV and film, I could not help but be drawn to the hit 2014 South Korean television drama, "Empress Gi" (*Gi Hwanghu*). This historical figure, who became the wife of the Mongol emperor in fourteenth-century China, arguably once stood as the most powerful person in the world, which was in stark contrast to her early life as an enslaved Korean sent to China as human "tribute."

The popularity of this drama, however, clearly disturbed some people in Korea who took their history seriously, for in the name of dramatic license, the show's writers and producers concocted preposterous storylines. In the early episodes, for example, the audience was supposed to believe that the then-young woman could have passed herself off as a swashbuckling *male* leader of a group of righteous bandits.

Actually, as a girl, the person who later became Empress Gi appears to have become ensnared in the periodic roundups of Korean female slaves bound for Mongol-controlled China during the latter part of the Goryeo era (tenth–fourteenth centuries). Once in the capital (present-day Beijing), she caught the eye of the Mongol emperor and became his favored concubine, and then his queen. When her husband eventually lost interest in governing, Lady ("Empress") Gi effectively took the throne, securing her power through the fact that her son was the crown prince.

Official Chinese and Korean histories, written by the succeeding Ming dynasty and the Joseon kingdom, respectively, portrayed her negatively and decried her abuse of power. The Korean records also detailed her intervention in Korean affairs from her perch in China and the venality of her family members, especially her brothers, in her homeland. Historians have questioned this starkly disparaging depiction of her in the official records, but the producers of the TV drama turned her into not only a complex and sympathetic figure but also a national hero in the struggles against Mongol domination. Rendering historical themes and events into nationalist allegories was certainly nothing new to the Korean entertainment industry, nor even to the Korean historical profession. But I would suggest that, in this case, the revisionism, though executed badly, might have been enlightening.

Like Viktor Ahn, the Korean-born short-track speed skater who won three gold medals for Russia in the 2014 Winter Olympics, Empress Gi can be considered a Korean who overcame the constraints of political circumstances to make her mark as a non-Korean. Though originally of Korean nationality or ethnicity—albeit a problematic notion when applied to the fourteenth century—Empress Gi transcended the boundaries of Korean-ness and thereby expanded the range of Korean influence and visibility beyond the peninsula. Viktor Ahn was celebrated by South Koreans for his successes, so why not Empress Gi?

Regardless of whether the makers of this drama ever thought in such terms, the example of Empress Gi reflects well the ongoing processes of globalization in South Korea, not only as a state and an economic powerhouse, but also as a society and a people. Furthermore, just as the hit makers of TV dramas, movies and pop music in the "Korean wave," also known as *Hallyu*, today spread South Korean popular culture to other parts of the world, Empress Gi once led a surge of interest in Korea as a source of exotic people and culture for China in the fourteenth century. She and other Korean travelers to China partook in the relatively open cultural exchange that was permitted by the singularly vast Mongol empire, which stretched from Korea in the East all the way to Europe in the West and included many civilizations in between, such as India, Persia and even Russia.

Back in the fourteenth century, in other words, Koreans not only spread their culture to far-flung places but also acquired the fruits of many other civilizations. This achievement is worth remembering today, as the content and very meaning of Korean identity have changed dramatically over the past two decades through the influx of immigrants and the country's increasing cultural interaction with the rest of the world.

Chapter 19

SPEAKING OF NORTHERN KOREA, NOT NORTH KOREA

So much attention is paid to North Korea and to the artificial national division implanted on the peninsula since the 1940s that we often overlook the geographical divisions that extend much further back in time. In fact, from the beginning, the balance between north and south on the peninsula has determined the character of "Korea" itself.

If we forgo the various origins myths, we can safely locate the cradle of Korean civilization in the Goguryeo kingdom, which appears to have begun about two thousand years ago in what is now Manchuria. Goguryeo extended its domain southward into the peninsula, but by the fourth-century CE, it ran up against states in the south like Baekje, whose rulers appear to have descended from Goguryeo, and Silla.

These three kingdoms later came to be viewed as part of a single national group, but that was a typical exercise of justifying the conquest of formerly different peoples. In language, culture and other features, the so-called "Three Kingdoms" were characterized by difference as much as commonality, and the strongest contrast appears to have been between the two southern kingdoms, on the one hand, and the northern kingdom of Goguryeo, on the other.

Silla's defeat of Baekje and then Goguryeo in the 660s brought about the first "unification" of the peninsula. But Silla's subsequent difficulties in driving out the Chinese, to whom it had turned for assistance in subduing the other two kingdoms, limited the area of its territorial seizure. In fact, most of the northern part of the peninsula came under the dominion of a kingdom, Balhae, whose leaders might have come from Goguryeo, but whose people were not recognized as the same as those of Silla and Baekje. This suggests again the distinctiveness of the southern civilizations from Goguryeo, which left the strongest imprint on the origins of Korean civilization.

These challenges of how to consider and integrate the northern areas were faced by both the "Unified Silla" kingdom and its successor state, Goryeo. But Goryeo's founder, Wang Geon, came from the west–central part of the peninsula and hence was keen on shifting the political heart of the country northward from Gyeongju in the southeast, which had been Silla's capital. Wang also turned to Goguryeo to name his own state, wanting to legitimize its status as the successor to both that former northern kingdom and to Silla. Wang did indeed extend the northern frontier from that of Silla's, but given the character of the social elites and political rulers, Korean civilization remained firmly grounded in the southern and central regions of the peninsula. And beyond that northern border lay people who were roundly viewed by Koreans as very different, even savage, for they launched attacks and invasion attempts throughout much of the Goryeo era.

When the Mongols finally succeeded in conquering Goryeo in the thirteenth century, they directly ruled the northern quarter of the country, which further pushed the northern regions outside the orbit of Korean rule. Interestingly, however, the north again came to shape the subsequent course of Korean history. General Yi Seong-gye, whose family had long served the Mongols on the northeastern fringe of Goryeo, overthrew his commanders and established his own dynastic rule, Joseon, at the end of the fourteenth century. Despite his roots and the influence of non-Koreans in his inner circle, however, Yi established his new capital along the central west coast, close to that of Goryeo's capital. Furthermore, the Joseon dynasty, for over a hundred years after its founding, endeavored to populate the newly claimed northern end of the peninsula, which Joseon took possession of in the wake of the Mongols' retreat.

These thousands of Korean settlers came from the south, but they were comprised of lower status groups, including criminals and slaves who were granted freedom in exchange for their move. All of this signaled the continuing power of the south–central elites, who mostly remained in their roles, even in the new dynastic order. Indeed, the previously long history of the north as a frontier area of shifting borders and violent confrontations, and its more recent history as the land of people with military, criminal, low status and even foreign backgrounds, rendered the northern half of Joseon a backwater.

This, at least, was the prevailing perspective among the dominant families of the southern and central areas, including the capital of Seoul. Such a prejudice resulted in political and social discrimination against northern peoples throughout the Joseon era, despite what appeared as signs of their significant cultural development. The north, in fact, achieved in some ways a more vibrant society and economy than the south in the latter half of the Joseon era, and their exclusion from the centers of power and prestige probably made them more receptive to external influence beginning in the nineteenth century.

At the turn of the twentieth century, the northern regions took the lead in establishing modern schools, while Pyeongan province, in the northwest, became the center of Protestant Christianity, the effects of which are still

Figure 19.1 Replica of the stele, in Manchuria, commemorating the exploits of King Gwanggaeto of Goguryeo, in front of the War Memorial Museum, Seoul.

being felt today in South Korea. And in a stunning irony, given their long history as a perceived backwater, the northern areas produced most of the major figures who established the foundations of modern Korean culture in the early twentieth century. Whether this long history of marginalization from the mainstream of Korea's historical development had anything to do with North Korea, however, remains an open question.

Part IV

DYNASTIC DEPTHS

Chapter 20

CURRENCY AND NATIONAL IDENTITY

Figure 20.1 The four South Korean paper bills, featuring (clockwise from top left) Toegye (Yi Hwang), King Sejong the Great, Sin Saimdang and Yulgok (Yi I).

Almost everyone thinks about money to a certain extent, but how often do people think about the symbols that they see on their coins and bills? For students of history, the images on currency, particularly of people, provide fascinating insight into a country's or a civilization's history—or more accurately, into how the people of a certain nation view their history.

A cursory survey around the world shows what most observers would suspect—that revered political leaders, military heroes, great scientists and famous cultural figures from the past usually appear on the currencies. Granted, the money in countries with autocratic leaderships, such as China or North Korea, often features recent or current dictators who are the objects of personality cults. But in most other places, the figures on the currency encapsulate what the people want to emphasize about their shared culture and hence serve as mirrors of contemporary sentiments and values. They are meant to reflect, in sum, a sense of unity and commonality.

Figure 20.2 Statue of Yulgok, Ojukheon Museum, Gangneung, South Korea.

This explains, perhaps, why the Queen of England is featured so prominently on the currencies not only of the United Kingdom but of other Commonwealth countries, which understandably has become a point of contention. Such sentiments, then, also tend to change over time, and currencies often reflect this by changing the faces that appear on them.

In South Korea, however, what is striking is the continuity of the historical figures showcased on its coins and banknotes. In the 1950s, the image of then-President Syngman Rhee was featured on the bills, which said more about Rhee and his dictatorial rule than any sense of history at the time. But since the 1960s and 1970s, three main figures from the past have graced the currency: Admiral Yi Sun-sin, King Sejong the Great, and the great scholar Yi I, or Yulgok. The philosopher Yi Hwang, or Toegye, joined this group in the early 1980s, and finally, in the late 2000s, a fifth figure appeared, Lady Shin Saimdang, an artist and, interestingly, the mother of Yulgok.

When the Bank of (South) Korea announced that the new 50,000-*won* banknote would feature Lady Shin, there was an outcry, but not because a woman had finally been selected, since it was known for a while that this would happen. Rather, the objections were that the Bank had chosen the wrong woman. They claimed that it should have been someone like Yu Gwan-sun, a celebrated martyr killed by Japanese colonial police as she was rallying her hometown for the March First Independence Movement of 1919. As with the people on prominent display in many other countries' currencies, Yu would have carried the proper credentials of the modern nationalist hero. Furthermore, those who protested the Bank's decision decried Lady Sin's standing as representative not of modern Korea, when women have become more socially liberated, but rather of the traditionally Confucian-dominated Korea when women were praised only for their subservient roles in relation to men. Despite her artistic accomplishments, Lady Shin seemed to have been selected mostly because she was a great philosopher's mother.

If we move beyond this debate on the relative merits of Lady Shin and Yu Gwan-sun, what is perhaps even more remarkable is that all four historical figures on the South Korean currency come from a single 200-year period in the history of one of the world's oldest civilizations. All five lived and died in the window between approximately 1400 and 1600—roughly the first two centuries of the Joseon era. What was it about this period that produced so many great historical figures? Or more accurately, what was it about this period that produced so many *safe* historical figures, free from controversy (notwithstanding the protest over Lady Shin)? And what was it about these four people that they could be readily appropriated for this honor?

Leaving aside the details of the political and other processes that led to their selections, it seems that we should start by noting that all four came from an era sufficiently removed from today, but not too much. That is, they are old enough to escape entanglement in contemporary historical controversies over the painful process of modern change in Korea. After all, what uniformly recognized major historical figure of the modern era could pass the test of holding pristine nationalist credentials while reflecting a consensus about contemporary values in a democratic South Korea? Just as importantly, these four figures' lives were not so far in the past that they have nothing to do with Korea today. They lived in an era when Confucianism, the all-encompassing social ethos that still pervades much of South Korean society, gradually became the dominant ideological and cultural marker of Korean civilization.

Of course, there is still another possibility—that this is simply a coincidence. After all, King Sejong the Great, Korea's most acclaimed cultural figure, and

Admiral Yi Sun-sin, its most celebrated military hero, would have been logical choices regardless of when they lived. But historians generally do not like to engage in contingencies. We like to find connectable patterns, especially those that link the past to the present and speak to fundamental issues, such as the role of history in national identity.

Chapter 21

CONCUBINE DESCENDANTS

If concubinage can be considered one of the more durable, consequential and interesting practices of Korean civilization, the historical significance of concubines' children and descendants, or *seoja*, in the traditional social and family system was even greater.

In the Joseon era (fourteenth to nineteenth centuries), particularly toward the latter half, the seoja (or *seoeol* or *seopa*, two other common terms, though with slightly different nuances) comprised a large population, which is understandable, given that concubinage itself was a widespread custom. What forged these concubines' descendants into a distinctive social status group was the legal discrimination and accompanying social prejudice against them. Due to the particular way Korean officials in the early Joseon dynasty chose to interpret Confucian teachings, the seoja, along with the descendants of remarried widows and other "unchaste" women, became prohibited from taking the state civil service examination. This effectively blocked the path toward the singular elite calling in the country, government office, and enabled the spread of this discrimination into other social realms, including the family.

That concubines' children held a lower status within their own households made for very awkward and unhappy circumstances. And despite the lack of any legal basis, the seoja were denied becoming successors to their fathers' lineages, as adoption of nephews for this purpose gradually became the norm. One can imagine the pain that this caused these children, a trauma that undoubtedly was passed down to their own descendants along with their social stigma. Indeed such difficulties became expressed in some of the most renowned folk tales of the Joseon era.

The "Tale of Hong Gil-dong," for example, features the concubine's son of a powerful official who runs away from home and eventually leads a group of righteous bandits. And the most famed story of all, the "Tale of Chunhyang," centers on a seoja girl whose hardships begin with the social expectations of being a courtesan's daughter. Despite these prejudices, however, some seoja eventually emerged as figures of great accomplishment and influence. (One assumes that, despite the bias, the odds of this happening gradually increased, given their swelling numbers.) Heo Jun, praised as Korea's greatest medical innovator and the author of "Dongui Bogam" (Encyclopedia of Korean Medicine), was a seoja who lived in the sixteenth and seventeenth centuries. And in the eighteenth century emerged Bak Je-ga, one of the core members of the Northern Learning School who laid out a systematic analysis of Joseon's social ills, based on economic principles. Bak Je-ga was also one of the Royal Library's (Gyujanggak) renowned "four librarians" of seoja status appointed directly by one of the great sage kings of Joseon, Jeongjo.

This is actually where the story of the seoja gets even more interesting. For Jeongjo himself was a seoja, as were his two predecessors and indeed, all of his successors to the throne for the rest of the Joseon dynasty. In an extraordinary irony, every Joseon monarch from 1720 to 1910, or nearly the last two of the five centuries of that longest running of Korea's dynastic reigns, was a concubine's descendant. This is because, like King Jeongjo, they were all, with one exception, the descendants of King Yeongjo, who reigned from 1724 to 1776.

The exception was King Gyeongjong, Yeongjo's older half-brother, but he too, like Yeongjo, was the son of a lower status concubine who happened to catch the eye of their father, King Sukjong. Gyeongjong, perhaps due to the childhood stress of living through the execution of his mother, Jang Huibin, survived less than five years on the throne (1720–1724) before his death. Yeongjo, who succeeded him, had to surmount vocal challenges to his legitimacy due to suspicions that he had actually poisoned his half-brother. But likely just as damaging was Yeongjo's status, too, as an "illegitimate" son.

In more than fifty years as king, Yeongjo eventually overcame both of these strikes against him and turned into what most historians consider one of the greatest Joseon monarchs. One has to wonder, however, how much the strains of battling the questions over his legitimacy affected his approach to rule, and how much this tormented him in his private life. These issues became dramatized in the recent film, "Sado" ("The Throne"), which depicts the searing psychological struggles in Yeongjo's relationship to his troubled son, whom he put to death by confining him to a rice chest. Notwithstanding this notoriously tragic episode, Yeongjo did as much as anyone to bring greater fairness to the political realm, by weakening the legal and institutional discrimination that had long victimized concubines' descendants (like himself).

This approach continued with his successor, his grandson Jeongjo, but in mirroring the fate of the long-running seoja effort to overcome their stigma, such reforms soon weakened once Jeongjo died. This was despite the fact that his successors in the nineteenth century were technically all seoja themselves. As monarchs, they were of course never referred to this way (at least openly), but it is somehow fitting that this identity, a social and legal construct, pervaded not only the masses but the royal family as well.

Chapter 22

THE REAL LIVES OF GISAENG COURTESANS

The people most commonly associated with romantic love in Korean folklore are the *gisaeng* courtesans, and the popular impression of their glamor and beauty appears to have taken shape through famous paintings and appealing tales from the late Joseon era.

Their beginnings date much further back, however, and their role in the social and cultural development of the country was significant, all the way to recent times. The gisaeng appear to have originated in the early Goryeo era (935–1392), and as they would until the twentieth century, their main identities were as government servants, in the sense not of civil service but rather of hereditary bondage. This low social status reflected their official duties to government officials and their guests: artistic performances as well as sexual services.

The further institutionalization of these multiple roles of subservience developed hand-in-hand with their growing significance as transmitters of Korean cultural forms in music, dance and literature. In the early Joseon era (1392–1897), the most famous gisaeng was Hwang Jini, from Gaeseong (or Songdo), the former capital of Goryeo, who was renowned for both her beauty and remarkably evocative poetry. Many of these poems survive to this day, and they speak powerfully to universal themes, including nature, sorrow, beauty and of course romantic love.

This somewhat strange and contradictory combination of roles placed the gisaeng in an odd social position: women who readily interacted with the most powerful but who belonged to, and were usually treated as, people whose social status barely rose above that of slaves. In fact, they were slaves, in that they rarely could escape their low birth status. They were also sexual slaves, due to the solidification of their role as concubines for the nobility and other highly privileged males. Very few children of these sexual unions, with fathers belonging to the uppermost level of society and mothers to the lowermost, could escape that stigma, although many of them tried.

This perhaps was an originating element behind the most famous Korean folk tale, the "Tale of Chunhyang." This story is often accepted as a sterling representation of Korean traditional culture, but it also symbolizes the multiple, contradictory and likely painful lives of the gisaeng. In the story, Chunhyang is the daughter of a former county magistrate of Namwon county, in Jeolla province, and of a local gisaeng. There was nothing unusual about such an existence, as there were likely many thousands of girls just like Chunhyang in real life. But in the story, the beautiful Chunhyang gets "married" to an aristocratic male and insists, in resisting the advances of another local magistrate, that she is not a gisaeng, unlike many other daughters of such unions who, in real life, indeed became gisaeng themselves. Indeed, the marriage union to a nobleman was highly unlikely in real Joseon society, as was the tale's happy ending.

Eventually, the Tale of Chunhyang, a story transmitted via oral traditions, became textualized as the libretto for a *pansori* opera, and then modernized as a short story through mass printing in the early twentieth century. The popularity of the tale grew and aroused a wide variety of perspectives, both literary and popular, on the details of the narrative and on its significance for understanding the place of gisaeng in Korean society and culture.

In the meantime, the gisaeng too modernized, as they became organized into associations that operated under the regulatory supervision of the state, including that of Japanese colonial rule (1910–1945). What resulted was a system of licensed prostitution that extended, in modified form, the customary connection between female subservience, "public service," and prostitution. This decidedly unglamorous combination could not have been unrelated to the so-called "comfort women" system of sexual bondage institutionalized by the Japanese empire in World War II.

After liberation in 1945, the gisaeng (though not the comfort women) disappeared from formal existence and practice. But the Tale of Chunhyang and other cultural artifacts related to the gisaeng underwent repeated embellishment and re-imaginings in popular culture through movies, television and theatrical stagings. In both North and South Korea, these courtesans from the past won elevation to status as national symbols. The intricate dances and musical performances that the gisaeng had collectively developed and transmitted came to be showcased as among the most beloved expressions of traditional Korean culture, just as Shin Yun-bok's beautiful eighteenth-century paintings of them also joined the pantheon of national artistic treasures.

All of these developments contributed to the formation of the gisaeng into the glittering representations of Korean folklore, art and romantic love. The city of Namwon, the location of the fictional folk tale, even constructed a Chunhyang theme park, where one can be surrounded by the famous places mentioned in the story and make believe that the enchanting world of gisaeng courtesans was real.

Chapter 23

A SHOCKING EXECUTION

Figure 23.1 Section of the wall of Suwon Fortress, originally built in the late eighteenth century to commemorate Prince Sado.

The only top political leader in Korea to remain in power longer than Kim Il-Sung, who commanded North Korea for nearly fifty years, was King Yeongjo, whose reign in the eighteenth century, from 1724 to 1776, actually passed the half-century mark. Like Kim, Yeongjo's long tenure allowed him to amass tremendous power. And he used this authority to advance a wide range of policies and practices that most scholars agree benefited the Joseon kingdom, which achieved a cultural peak amid political stability under his rule.

In the end, however, Yeongjo is most remembered for a family tragedy in which he played the leading role: His shocking execution of his own son, and in a manner that still elicits an unshakable sadness and bewilderment. Most Koreans eventually learn this story of Crown Prince Sado (Sado Seja) being forced into a rice chest, which was then sealed shut to ensure that he would wither away after several days. Not surprisingly, this remarkable event has often been captured in the popular imagination, such as through television dramas that have replayed this excruciating moment in different ways. And

Figure 23.2 Statue of King Jeongjo, Suwon Fortress, Suwon, South Korea.

recently a grand movie by director Lee Joon-ik, and starring no less than the great actor Song Gang-ho in the leading role, offered a retelling of "history's most tragic family incident" by focusing on the troubled personal relationship between father and son, between the monarch and his heir to the throne.

In the Joseon monarchy, the effects of even the most private family matters extended to the country as a whole, at times shaking the very foundations of the ruling system. This was why disputes over royal succession often resulted in violence and crises that engulfed the government and society. But until the execution of Sado, there had not been an incident in which the crown prince himself was not only demoted or punished, but killed by the same governing order led by his father.

People have long wondered what really triggered such a shocking event. Was the prince's unpredictable behavior, which admittedly was severe, indeed a menace to the entire country? Further, why did King Yeongjo feel the need to kill his son instead of sending him, for example, into exile? And why would Yeongjo choose such a gruesome, unbearably drawn-out manner of execution, as if he wanted to prolong his son's suffering? How could this possibly have been the action of a sagely monarch, which Yeongjo strived to be and is generally credited as having been?

These are just some of the mysteries behind this incident. And the answers, to varying degrees of believability, can be deduced from a number of documentary sources. They range from official government records, which hint at the deep-seated problems between father and son and political considerations that went into this decision, to personal observations that recount the incident in the context of family relations. The most famous unofficial account is "Hanjungnok," an autobiography written much later by the doomed prince's wife, Lady Hong. Her narrative tries as deftly as possible to explain how her husband went from being a strapping young man with tremendous promise to a deeply disturbed victim of mental illness.

Prince Sado's reckless killing of his servants and others around him made his conduct an urgent issue demanding a stern response. King Yeongjo, approaching seventy years of age, had to consider how the Joseon monarchy itself could continue following his own passing. And Yeongjo's decision to have his dangerous son killed probably stemmed from a concern that, short of a grim solution, the possibility of Sado's assuming power could remain a looming threat, perhaps even to Yeongjo's own reign and life.

Or perhaps Yeongjo was driven to this extreme action by political circumstances stemming from bitter rivalries among his officials, which understandably became the foremost conspiracy theory, as reflected in Yi In-hwa's novel, "Eternal Empire" (*Yeongwonhan Jeguk*). This story is set in the final days (one day, actually) of Yeongjo's grandson and successor, King Jeongjo, who was the son of Prince Sado. As a child of around 10, Jeongjo had to live through this horrific event in which his father was killed by his own grandfather. So as he ascended to the throne in 1776 in his mid-20s, Jeongjo had to abide by his formal loyalty to his preceding king and grandfather while muting what must have been unbearable personal torment and enormous resentment.

It is a wonder that Jeongjo did not fall victim to trauma and start to act erratically and dangerously himself, unleashing a torrent of rage while being consumed by a thirst for vengeance. But indeed, Jeongjo in his quarter century of rule seems to have prioritized the path of steady reform amid stability that had characterized much of his grandfather's reign.

Jeongjo also, however, gradually rehabilitated his father's name and standing. In 1795, after nearly two decades on the throne, and in celebration of the 60th birthdays of both his parents, Jeongjo led a lavish procession from Seoul to Suwon, to where he had moved his father's gravesite. There, a grand monument to his father was under construction: the Hwaseong Fortress that still today serves as a reminder of that extraordinary moment in history.

Part V

MODERN ORIGINS

Chapter 24

JUNGIN, FORERUNNERS TO PROFESSIONALS

One of the most interesting hereditary social groups of premodern Korea was a band of technical specialists called the *jungin* ("middle people"). During the latter half of the Joseon kingdom, the jungin carried out specialized, technical functions shunned by the better-known *yangban* nobility but nonetheless essential to the functioning of the government. They filled official posts responsible for interpreting, medicine, law, the sciences, accounting, document preparation and even painting.

The jungin who staffed the Office of Interpreters, for example, trained civil servants in foreign languages (Chinese, Mongolian, Manchu, and Japanese), devised state examinations and supplied government interpreters for the court. These interpreters, a select group that had to pass a competitive screening process to win appointment, translated documents, compiled textbooks and developed the curriculum for foreign language instruction. But the most prominent function of these interpreters was to represent the court and government in border localities such as Uiju and Busan, as well as outside the country by joining periodic diplomatic missions to China and Japan. This experience also provided opportunities to build wealth through trading.

Perhaps most importantly, their linguistic skills and exposure to the outside world supplied them with ideas, models and contacts that eluded most other Koreans, including the ruling aristocracy. This would prove particularly important to the jungin during the Korean enlightenment period beginning in the late nineteenth century. Among the most visible and influential jungin interpreters were those in the Hyeon family, which produced a veritable who's who of major figures of the early modern period. These people helped shape the wave of government and social reform characterizing the Korean enlightenment, ascended the bureaucratic ranks of the officialdom and contributed greatly to the emergence of a new elite and culture in modern Korea.

We can begin with Hyeon Chae, who at the turn of the twentieth century produced more than a dozen translations and textbooks on subjects ranging from history to Korean grammar. His works, in fact, represented a micro-cosm of the diverse intellectual trends among the cultural pioneers of this period. They employed the lessons of Social Darwinism, republicanism and other ideologies to further the cause of self-strengthening, Western education, Korean independence, and the awakening of the nation. More than any other traditional status group, it was the jungin who stood at the forefront of these fundamental, nearly revolutionary changes.

Another member of this extended family, Hyeon Jin-geon, became one of the preeminent authors of modern Korean literature. Like many other colonial era (1910–1945) writers, Hyeon Jin-geon attended school abroad, in Japan and China, before returning to Korea to work as a novelist and reporter. His works are renowned for their vividly realistic portraits of struggling Koreans learning to adjust to the rapidly changing world.

His second cousin, Hyeon Cheol, became one of the founders of modern Korean theater. He helped to establish a native theatrical tradition by organizing study societies, translating Western works to be staged in Korean, and founding performance schools. And, of course, he penned his own important contributions, in the form of both plays and criticism, to the fledgling Korean theater movement.

Another major cultural figure from this family was Hyeon Je-myeong, a versatile instrumentalist and one of the pioneers of Western music in Korea. He was later implicated, however, in what was considered pro-Japanese activities during the wartime mobilization of the late 1930s and early 1940s. This resulted from a difficult set of circumstances that ensnared many of the new social elite, including the jungin descendants, during the Japanese colonial period.

One of the most explicitly pro-Japanese Koreans, in fact, was Hyeon Yeong-seop, a public intellectual and educator. In the late 1930s, he published a book, "The Path Koreans Should Take," which argued that the Korean people could only be saved from their wretched political, family and social system by shedding their identities as Koreans and becoming Japanese in both mind and spirit.

But consider also Hyeon Yeong-seop's cousin, Hyeon Jun-seop, who under the name of Peter Hyun wrote a book called, "Man Sei! The Making of a Korean American." In this work, Peter Hyun detailed the struggles of his family as immigrants in the United States and the heroic work of his father, the reverend Hyeon Sun (Soon Hyun), an independence activist working to overthrow Japanese rule.

That two diametrically opposing perspectives on national identity in the modern world could come from cousins provides a good indication of the variety of ways the descendants of the Hyeon family, and of the jungin in general, made their mark on modern Korea. After centuries behind the scenes as practitioners of skills that were held in low esteem, they exploded onto the upper strata of government, religion, culture and education in the modern era.

In many ways, the jungin were the forerunners to modern professionals, so it was understandable that, based on their accumulated know-how and greater awareness of new ideas and models, they would make their mark as influential elites in the early twentieth century. Their ascendance to such prominence and social influence represented, then, not only a compelling story of modern social change, but the often hidden and potentially powerful features of premodern Korea as well.

Chapter 25

1894, A SIGNAL YEAR

In late July of 1894, a quick succession of events took place that overturned the old order in Korea, and eventually in East Asia as a whole. What began with the Japanese military's seizure of the Korean royal palace led soon to the Gabo Reforms, a series of fundamental changes decreeing a completely new form and direction for the government and overturning social and cultural norms that dated back centuries, if not millennia. Slavery, hereditary social status, discrimination against widows and concubines, and many other means of determining social privilege were formally abolished.

This did not mean that everything shifted overnight, however, as some of these reforms took years and even decades to realize. But the initiation and articulation of momentous change proved significant and durable, and the "spirit of Gabo" persisted as a driving force for social and political reform that shaped the subsequent emergence of modern Korea.

The Japanese had a lot to do with this, as their troops had enabled the Gabo Reforms to occur in the first place, and a decade later they returned, amid a war with Russia, to begin the colonization of Korea that would last until 1945. But back in 1894, the Japanese had little to do with the actual substance of the Gabo Reforms, which addressed deeply rooted problems that could only be identified and properly addressed by Koreans.

The Japanese also had a larger agenda: China. They were determined to topple China's domination over northeast Asia, a sphere of influence dating back thousands of years. The Japanese victory over the Qing dynasty in a war, which began in the summer of 1894 and was fought almost exclusively in Korea, flipped the traditional order of East Asia. It also facilitated Japan's empire building through the taking of Taiwan and parts of Manchuria as war booty in 1895, then Korea in the first decade of the twentieth century, the rest of Manchuria in the 1930s, and finally much of East and Southeast Asia, including China, in the 1940s. This half-century growth of Japanese imperialism, and of Japanese economic and cultural influence over the region, became arguably the dominant historical factor in East Asia in the modern era. And arguably it began in the streets of Seoul in July 1894.

But what brought the Japanese to Korea in the first place? This brings us to the third monumental event of that year, the one that started it all: the Donghak Uprising. Donghak, a native Korean religion founded in the early 1860s, had grown mostly underground in the intervening three decades, until its followers exploded onto the scene in the spring of 1894. They rebelled against the searing corruption of a county official in northern Jeolla province and soon captured most of the surrounding region. They defeated government troops sent down to pacify them, and the Korean court, justifiably feeling endangered, called China for help.

The quick entrance of Chinese troops into the battle against the Donghak rebels, though, came at a major cost to the Korean government, for this move also gave a reason for Japan to join the fray. The Japanese troops not only occupied the capital city in July, but they also used this position as the basis for formally launching a war against the Chinese, in a confrontation that had been brewing since the early 1880s. The ensuing devastation to the Korean countryside, especially in the northern regions, was enormous, which was gruesomely fitting, because the Japanese and Chinese were ultimately fighting for control over Korea.

The outcomes of both this Sino-Japanese War and the Gabo Reforms ensured the end of China's unrivaled influence in Korea, which in some form or another dated back over a millennium years. So what began as a revolt against local corruption in a small corner of the peninsula in the spring of 1894 triggered a chain of events whose consequences extended to the greater East Asian region and the rest of modern East Asian history. And through the Gabo Reforms, the impact of 1894 on Koreans' own efforts to modernize was pivotal.

Yet, among these three major events of 1894, what Koreans today most commemorate is the Donghak Uprising. Part of this stems from the Gabo Reforms' association with Japan, and Koreans understandably find that unsettling, given Japan's domineering role in the nation's subsequent history. And the war between Japan and China, likewise, is seen as the first of several modern battles over Korea between menacing imperialist powers that stripped the country of its independence and dignity. The Donghak Uprising, on the other hand, is credited with defending the common people against injustice and thereby serving as a model for righteous social movements throughout modern Korean history. Just as important, the Donghak Uprising, which began with domestic goals but soon morphed into an anti-foreign crusade as well, is perceived as a great example of Koreans' struggle for national self-determination against the ravages of foreign interference.

Figure 25.1 Bronze statue of Jeon Bongjun, leader of the Donghak forces of 1894, next to a subway entrance, downtown Seoul.

Depending on one's background or interests, one could argue for any of these three major events from 1894 as being the most important. But there is no denying that, together, all three contributed to making that year the signal moment in the birth of modern Korea.

Chapter 26

GREAT KOREAN EMPIRE

Over the past couple of decades, the common perspective on the Great Korean Empire (Daehan Jeguk), which began in 1897 and ended when Japan annexed Korea as a colony in 1910, has changed almost completely. Historians, followed by the public at large, have revived the reputation of the Empire, which had long been derided as the last breath of the dying Joseon dynasty and beset by disorder, corruption and mismanagement.

It is easy to see why the Japanese condemned the Korean Empire: Such a narrative of hopeless backwardness and dangerous weakness justified Japan's takeover, which was legitimized in terms of regional security and urgent reform, as if Japan was forced to intervene. But many Koreans back then and long afterward also shared this negative view; it was the Empire, after all, that had "lost" the country through its inability to respond to the times. It must have been incompetent.

Recently, however, scholars have found reason to uphold the Great Korean Empire as a bold attempt to lead the nation toward modern change. Indeed the 1897 founding appears to have been motivated by a desire to escape Chinese, Japanese and Russian interference by establishing Korea on equal footing with these surrounding, menacing powers. Such a move, then, followed in the footsteps of the sweeping Gabo Reforms of 1894–1895, which had formally ended Korea's centuries-long subordinate relationship with China.

The renovating spirit of the Gabo Reforms continued in other ways as well. The Empire's Royal Household Ministry and particularly its treasury, the Office of Crown Properties, pursued a comprehensive set of modernizing innovations. They included the government-sponsored construction, in 1899, of the first railway line and the Seoul streetcar system, as well as developmental projects in mining, commerce and trade, electricity generation, waterworks, and communication infrastructure such as the telegraph network.

Meanwhile, for its part the central government, which lay outside the Royal Household Ministry, also led modernization efforts, despite being weaker financially and bureaucratically than the Crown. These steps included implementing a new household registration system in order to streamline government management of the population, as well as a nationwide land survey in order to standardize ownership and enhance taxation methods. The government also pursued measures to improve public schooling, strengthen public health and nurture patriotic sentiment.

In sum, the Korean Empire worked to build and fortify Korea's nationhood and material well-being, which paralleled similar efforts in broader society, especially by "enlightenment" activists who championed modernization, reform and independence. There was much to suggest, in other words, that Korea was not in such bad shape, certainly not bad enough to warrant conquest.

So what went wrong? Why did the Korean Empire fall into status as a Japanese colony, a process that began in 1904 and ended in 1910? The short answer, of course, is that Japanese imperialism was simply too strong militarily, economically and diplomatically. The long answer, though, is much more complicated, and there is no consensus among historians, despite the recent scholarly emphasis on the Korean Empire's strengths, as described above. Indeed one of the unavoidable realities is that many Koreans, both elite and non-elite, actually helped the Japanese in the takeover process, which upsets the straightforward impression of Korea's being ruined by the evil forces of Japanese imperialism.

As pointed out by historians who deny the rosier picture of the Korean Empire, there was a good reason for Koreans at the time, and for many decades thereafter, to question the Empire's supposed advances. Gojong, the monarch whose conventional image has been reversed by the recent revisionist scholarship, actually was considered a stumbling block to reform by the enlightenment activists of the period. Their fears were realized soon after the founding of the Korean Empire, as Emperor Gojong shut down the reformist Independence Club because of its calls for a more constitutional, accountable form of government.

Around the same time, in 1899, Gojong and his closest advisors, who appear to have operated largely in the shadows, also issued a formal declaration of the Empire's "state system." This edict established the five-centuries-old Joseon dynasty as the basis of the Empire's legitimacy while pronouncing that just about every sphere of government and society now lay under the monarch's unquestioned control. Such royal absolutism was not uncommon around the world and considered by some a sign of modernity and strength, but it also showed how the Empire contained many despotic, regressive and debilitating elements and tendencies.

Still, because its end, and that of Korean sovereignty, came at the hands of the Japanese, the Empire can readily be shown as a tragic victim, despite its spirited demonstration of Koreans' quest for independence and advancement.

The new prevailing historical view portrays the Empire as having established a basis for achieving autonomous modern change, and it would have, had the Japanese not robbed the Koreans of this potential. As a source of historical inspiration, then, the Great Korean Empire's accomplishments are now celebrated despite its short life, and among its long-term fruits is the formal name, "Daehan Minguk," of South Korea itself.

Chapter 27

MARCH FIRST INDEPENDENCE MOVEMENT

Figure 27.1 Pagoda Park, site of the initial public reading of the March First Declaration of Independence, downtown Seoul.

Every year Koreans commemorate the March First Independence Movement of 1919, celebrated as a testament to the yearning for freedom from Japanese colonial rule. An annual rite to mark the start of spring, solemn observances and colorfully staged reenactments around the country simulate the nation-wide eruption of demonstrations back in 1919.

Figure 27.2 Reenactment of March First demonstrations on the grounds of a local high school, March 1, 2012, Busan, South Korea.

Ironically, March First might actually have represented the last such moment of great unity, bringing together Koreans from all across the peninsula for a single cause. For various reasons, Koreans under colonial rule did not, or could not, organize another concerted action for independence, and as we know, the liberation of 1945 was immediately followed by Korea's permanent division. But while March First did not immediately bring about Korean autonomy, when viewed over the longer term, its historical significance was wide-ranging and monumental, especially in facilitating Koreans' central role in forging their own modern history.

March First showed the outcome of several decades of schooling and civic discourse concerning enlightenment and social reform, which heightened the sense of national unity as well as the thirst for independence. Throughout the modern world, often it took a common threat or domination by an external force to spark or intensify a sense of national identity, and Korea was no different. It came too late to prevent colonization, but March First showed that Koreans had developed a strong collective consciousness and will.

Such resolve was demonstrated within a month after the uprisings, as independence activists gathered in Shanghai, China in April 1919 to form the first government in exile, which significantly took the form of a republic, not a monarchy. Alas, this unity among the participants did not last long, as soon the independence movement split into disparate groups following competing ideologies and scattered in various locales, from China and Manchuria to even Japan and the United States.

These independent independence movements, however, would eventually cultivate the major political leaders, from Kim Il-Sung to Gim Gu and Syngman Rhee, who would take command over Korea's future course by the middle of the twentieth century. None of them played a major role in bringing about liberation, but their efforts in organizing anti-Japanese resistance movements from their far-flung bases outside the peninsula were enough to endow them with the stamp of nationalist legitimacy. In this sense, they were all the children of March First, and in fact the South Korean state, led by Rhee upon its founding in 1948, explicitly pointed to March First and the Shanghai Provisional Government of 1919 as the foundational basis of its existence.

There was another way that March First had a major historical impact, however, beyond sparking the liberation movements and the spirit of resistance. The demonstrations, which began with the reading of a declaration of independence as people gathered in Seoul to attend the funeral of the former Korean monarch, Gojong, induced a severely violent response from the colonial authorities, but eventually, also a major turn in colonial rule. The protests represented the explosion of discontent over the first decade of Japanese rule, which had been dominated by concerns over security (stamping out armed and other resistance) and therefore imposed all kinds of restrictions on Koreans' lives. Still, the Japanese rulers were shocked by the scale and scope of the unrest once it began, and this contributed to the terrible violence that met the demonstrators.

But the lessons from both the protests and their botched suppression fell on receptive ears amid a liberalizing political atmosphere back in Japan. What resulted was a new colonial administration installed in the fall of 1919, which declared the overarching policy of "cultural rule" that valued the "harmony of Japan and Korea" as the centerpiece of colonial administration. This did not mean, of course, that Koreans would be granted independence; indeed the ensuing reforms, taken together, probably had the effect of actually strengthening Japanese domination. The period of "cultural rule" maintained the larger mechanisms of authoritarian control, such as censorship and restrictions on political activity by organizations such as the communist party, and the colonial regime continued to rely on ethnic discrimination and segregation to maintain foreign rule.

Koreans, however, were now able to participate much more freely in publishing, religion, business and other social realms, and what resulted was an explosion in associational activity, as people gathered in groups dedicated to all kinds of cultural and economic endeavors. In the countryside, life continued largely as before, but the rapidly growing urban areas displayed a noticeably different, modern way of life.

Cultural Rule, a byproduct of March First, continued into the 1930s until it was overwhelmed by the total mobilization for Japan's pursuit of the Pacific War, the excesses of which would forever mark how Koreans remembered the colonial experience as a whole. In the end, one can debate whether the reforms of the 1920s signaled a "successful" outcome of March First. But the major changes that followed the uprising represented another example of how Koreans directly shaped their modern existence, and for that, March First should indeed be celebrated.

Chapter 28

THE POLITICS OF DISEASE

The anxious public response to the South Korean government's handling of the Middle East Respiratory Syndrome (MERS) outbreak in 2015 reminded us that South Koreans, like most people around the world, assume several things. First, they expect the government, or the state, to take responsibility for controlling infectious diseases. Second, they believe that only the government can undertake such an assignment, because it requires enormous resources as well as the power to restrict people's movement and behavior. Despite the advanced bureaucratic management of medicine during the Joseon dynasty, such public expectations formed mostly in the modern era.

And this gets us to the third major assumption that citizens hold in the face of an epidemic: The legitimacy of the government, especially its leadership, rests on how well it performs in containing or preventing damage. This is why the state response in these circumstances easily becomes politicized. There is, of course, a compelling history behind all this—not only of the state's public health and disease control measures, but also of the relationship between this administrative performance and political legitimacy. To illustrate, we can focus on two pioneering medical scientists who also happened to work for the government.

The first is Ji Seog-yeong, of the late nineteenth to early twentieth centuries. Ji has traditionally been credited as the first Korean to devise, apply and propagate vaccination treatments for smallpox. He was trained in techniques introduced by foreigners in Korea, especially the Japanese in Busan in the 1880s and 1890s. And as a county magistrate in the Busan area in the mid-1890s, he further developed and implemented these treatments.

By then Ji's activities were part of a larger push by the Korean government, beginning with the Gabo Reforms of 1894–1895, to establish a scientific disease-control system. The first major test came in the summer of 1895, as an outbreak of cholera, in the wake of the Sino-Japanese War in northern Korea, began to ravage that region and started to head south toward the capital. The Korean government hurriedly mobilized central and local officials, including the police, as well as doctors and foreign advisors, to contain the disease's destructive impact. While the victims eventually numbered in the

Figure 28.1 Ji Seog-yeong (courtesy of *The Korea Times*).

Figure 28.2 Baek In-je (*The Korea Times*).

hundreds, it could have been a lot worse, and it was generally considered a successful government response that heightened the public's view of the Gabo government's legitimacy, at least momentarily.

The succeeding Great Korean Empire, or *Daehan Jeguk*, built on these experiences and further developed both the state's understanding and bureaucratic organization for dealing with contagions. This came in handy when, in 1902, another cholera outbreak hit. So devastating had cholera become (as it was in other parts of the world as well), that when the Japanese conquered Korea beginning in 1905, they made cholera prevention, and disease control in general, one of the major priorities of their rule.

This also entailed, however, a denial of preceding Korean efforts, for such a narrative helped legitimate the Japanese takeover itself. This uncomfortable reality subsequently affected historical perceptions as well. In more recent times, the conventional understanding even of Ji's contributions has been criticized by Korean scholars as a product of Japanese propaganda that exaggerated his dependence on Japanese training. This seems to go too far, however. Ji, after all, was no pro-Japanese figure; he is better known, in fact, as one of the great advocates of the propagation and systematization of the Korean alphabet in the early twentieth century. But we see through this example how large the stakes can become when setting the narratives of political legitimacy and government performance concerning medicine and disease control.

This point is further illustrated by the life and ultimate fate of another great Korean medical pioneer, Baek In-je. Baek became one of the first licensed Korean physicians under Japanese colonial rule. But more importantly, he made heralded advancements in medical and surgical techniques, worked in the colonial government hospital, earned a doctorate from Tokyo University's Medical School and became one of the very few Korean professors in the Seoul Medical College. He also established his own clinic, which eventually became the famed Baek Hospital of Seoul and Busan. Near Busan, Baek In-je's son and nephew also founded a prestigious medical school called, fittingly, Inje University.

What further heightened Baek In-je's historical significance, however, was his tragic end. In the opening weeks of the Korean War in the summer of 1950, both he and his younger brother, Baek Bung-je, were captured by North Korean forces and taken north, never to be heard from again. The North Koreans targeted social elites like the Baek brothers who had worked in the colonial government, considering them all national traitors. But Baek In-je was a doctor and scientist who was driven by the physician's creed of providing medical care, regardless of whether this care came through a Japanese or Korean institution.

To the North Koreans, however, Baek's contributions were tainted because the entire colonial order was illegitimate (and worse), and hence anyone connected to Japanese rule was a criminal. This issue of how to treat Koreans associated with the colonial system remains a sensitive topic in South Korea, and it highlights the often uneasy but understandable connection between politics and medicine in modern Korean history.

Chapter 29

KOREAN UNIVERSITIES

The history of higher education in Korea is, depending on how one defines it, either remarkably long or surprisingly short. In the late fourteenth century, the new Joseon kingdom established an academy for aspirants to government office, where they could study for the state's civil service examination. However, this training center, called Seonggyungwan, had a curriculum limited to Confucian ethics and philosophy; it lacked a program to teach the arts, administration, practical sciences and technical specialties, which were taught by other schools. It would be difficult, in other words, to recognize the Seonggyungwan as a university, despite claims by the current Sungkyunkwan University of a history of over 600 years.

As a modern institution, the Seonggyungwan, in fact, began at the turn of the twentieth century, when it, along with schools with names like Yonhi, Severance, Sookmyung, Ewha and Bosung, was established to meet the needs of specialized education beyond the secondary level. In the subsequent period of Japanese colonial rule (1910–1945), these schools, which became the forerunners to well-known universities later, joined the many institutions of higher learning that, much like technical colleges, specialized in fields such as medicine, theology and women's education. There was, however, one recognizable university in the colonial period, Keijo Imperial University in Seoul ("Keijo" in Japanese), which was founded in the mid-1920s. This university, though, was built not to serve as an open-access public institution of higher education, but rather to cater to the hundreds of thousands of Japanese settlers, as well as to a relatively small number of Koreans.

Following liberation in 1945, this configuration of one university and many specialty colleges developed into the array of universities in South Korea that we see today. Under the American occupation (1945–1948), for example, Keijo Imperial University became the basis for the formal establishment of Seoul National University (SNU) in 1946. (This connection to the colonial past is understandably a sensitive topic, so in its official narrative SNU has simply erased this part of its history.) More troubling than the Japanese connection, however, and for reasons that defy easy understanding, SNU, along with Korea University (the descendant of Bosung College) and Yonsei University (the joint descendant of Yonhi College and Severance Medical School), somehow became entrenched as the "top three" universities in prestige and power. So dominant did these three schools become in higher education, and hence also in the education system as a whole, that in popular parlance they collectively took on the English acronym of "SKY" (SNU, Korea, Yonsei) to reflect the heavenly loftiness of their standing.

Unfortunately for South Korean society, they also represented the rigidity and restrictions of the university system. They became perched atop both official and unofficial rankings that, when married to the university entrance examination system and the hiring practices of governments and corporations, consigned over 90 percent of all aspiring college students to second-class status. The exclusionary practices and culture centered in these three schools, particularly SNU, were not limited to their admissions process. SNU, for example, chose almost solely from among its own graduates when hiring professors, to a shocking extent given that this was supposed to be a public university. Not surprisingly, Yonsei and Korea Universities came to view their own practices of hiring mostly their own graduates as a means of protecting themselves from the fallout of SNU's example. Other universities, then, had no choice but to follow suit, and so on. One is tempted to call this a cycle of abuse.

Abuse is an apt term for the horrible impact of this rigidly hierarchical university system through its perpetuation of the college entrance "examination hell," which robbed teenagers of their adolescence and effectively judged nearly all educated South Koreans on a single moment in their young lives. Those belonging to the overwhelming majority of the test takers who could not enter one of the designated prestigious universities were thereafter permanently restricted in their life and career possibilities.

The absurdity and abomination of such a system, especially in cultivating a democratic society, have been recognized at least since the 1990s, when astute social commentators began to call for the closing of SNU. They realized that the edifice of the university hierarchy, along with its attendant abuses and negative effects throughout society, could never be torn down without the elimination of SNU itself. This was a school, after all, that was founded by Japanese colonizers as an exclusionary institution. But while public anxiety surrounding this very broad and systematic problem has only increased with time, nothing has been done to fundamentally alter this order.

Here we encounter the entrenched structural impediment to real reform: Those who have benefited most from this system, the graduates of the SKY schools, occupy the most powerful and influential positions in South Korean society, including in the realms of politics and law, the state bureaucracy, the press, and yes, education. They would have to awaken to the larger social harm of the system that protects their privileges. This seems unlikely to happen.

Part VI

CHALLENGES OF NATIONHOOD

Chapter 30

KOREA'S PAST IN LIGHT OF BREXIT

The lingering aftermath of the so-called Brexit, or British exit from the European Union (EU), reminds us again of the power of nationalism. A complex mix of concerns seems to have driven the vote in 2016 to leave the European common market, but at its core was the resurgence of English nationalism.

The mostly older Englishmen and women who chose to regain full autonomy from Europe seem to have disregarded, however, the fact that Great Britain itself is very much a conglomerate of nations, a mini-EU. Somehow they believed that what they practiced in the United Kingdom could not be tolerated in England's relationship to greater Europe. It was also clear that most people of Scotland and Northern Ireland wanted to stay in the EU. They had, after all, become accustomed to such an arrangement for hundreds of years while retaining their national identities. Now the question is whether the Scots and Irish can remain in the United Kingdom if they cannot stay in the EU.

There is no easy solution to harmonizing such a wide range of concerns from various sides, especially the consequences of globalization and its accompanying migration patterns, but the growing sentiment seems headed toward ever-stronger nationalism in Europe and other places, including, as we have seen, the United States.

For South Korea, it is not clear what the immediate consequences will be, but these trends and Brexit call to mind the major moments in Korean history when Koreans, too, had to reconsider their collective standing within a larger political or cultural sphere, and therefore had to reframe their sense of national identity.

Of course, for most Koreans throughout history, one's group identity was largely limited to the extended family and village, or perhaps to the local region. They probably had little sense of "Korea" beyond knowing, or hearing, that in the faraway capital there was a king who presided over a larger realm populated by others who likely spoke the same language, followed similar customs, and fell under the same governing system. What continues to be a point of historical debate and ongoing research is precisely when this vague sense of collectivity sharpened into something more powerful and coherent, a sentiment that mirrored the learned elites' formulation of a separate Korean identity.

Whatever the answer, it is probable that such a sense of national identity trailed considerably the unity enforced by government administration and military conquests, such as the Silla "unification" in the seventh century or the Goryeo reunification of the peninsula in the tenth. But politics, and especially invasions from the outside, also played a central role in triggering such national integration. For example, the long siege by various northern neighbors, such as the Khitan, Jurchen or Mongols, during the Goryeo era clearly made Korean social and cultural elites, at least, determined to distance themselves from such "barbarians," at least until the long period of Mongol domination further complicated such feelings.

Similarly, textual evidence from the approximately half-century period in the mid-Joseon era, from the Japanese invasions of the 1590s to the Manchu invasions of the 1630s, shows a growing sense of collective identity spreading down to the common people. This makes sense because the commoners and lower status groups both suffered the most from, and contributed the most in repelling or overcoming, these invasions.

Within the ruling class, what seems to have stimulated even more thinking about Koreas' place in the larger realm of East Asia, particularly in relation to China, was the fall of China itself through the Manchus' conquest of the Ming dynasty in 1644. Thereafter, many Korean scholars and officials argued that only Korea remained as a proper civilization, by which they meant Confucian civilization. They furthermore believed that, in defense of this standing, Koreans must adjust their long-standing perception of China as the center of high culture, including their obligations and other ties to the continent. Similar motives had lain behind England's secession from Catholic Europe in the mid-sixteenth century. Koreans did not go so far as to establish a new religious order like the Anglican Church, but in other ways, they further emphasized their distinctive cultural identity from China, now under the control of the Manchus but still exercising a political, or at least diplomatic, supremacy over the peninsula.

This separation from the greater East Asian cultural sphere, centered on the continent, took its final, dramatic step in the late nineteenth century, when the geopolitical forces of imperialism ravaged the region, including eventually Korea. But Korea's divorce from China, at least politically, came at the hands of Japanese imperialist interests, which ultimately resulted in Japan's takeover of Korea in the early twentieth century. This drawn-out process, however, compelled Koreans, both elite and commoner, to further develop their understanding and beliefs about their collective identity in relation to larger, often menacing, outside forces.

Such an attempt took place throughout the period of Japanese colonial rule, from 1910 to 1945. And Koreans received another jolt after liberation in 1945, when they immediately became dominated by a new world order, the Cold War, that forced them into an often contentious debate (among South Koreans, anyway) about their relationship to the region and to the world at large. We are still living under those circumstances, and as with Brexit, we await the long-term consequences of that discussion.

Chapter 31

OPENNESS AND EXCLUSION

One of the most fascinating and distinctive features of Korean society in the past was that, for over a millennium, privilege and rank were determined by a complex mixture of openness and exclusion. As in most cultures, a very small number of people, particularly the monarchy and aristocracy, dominated political power and access to resources by exploiting the mass of commoners and slaves. Who belonged in these categories, of course, was based on the accident of birth.

There was, though, also an element of openness in granting privilege: the state examinations to select government officials. Such practices reflected mostly the influence of Confucian teachings, which increased in Korea as time passed. But Confucianism valued stability and hierarchy even more, and in Korea, this combination of both the open and the closed produced an enduring supremacy of the nobility, commonly known as the "yangban." These and other elites passed down, generation after generation, their privileged and exclusive access to educational benefits and political favors.

Beginning in the late nineteenth century, however, Korean leaders were forced to reconsider not only whether such a system was fair or morally acceptable, but also whether it produced the kind of country that could survive in the modern world. These concerns, expressed by such notable figures as Yu Gil-jun and Seo Jae-pil (Philip Jaisohn), introduced the now conventional notion of categorizing Korea and other countries as "advanced," "backward," or something in between. They understood that a vital criterion for becoming advanced or "enlightened" was the degree of openness and fairness in assigning social, economic and political privileges. Although such new ideas were adopted by government officials and public intellectuals alike, throughout the modern era there remained a tension between the pursuit of such openness and the pull of traditional Confucian values. Confucian ideals, furthermore, were not all incompatible with the goals of developing a modern society. The great importance attached to learning, for example, would provide a solid basis for rewarding intelligence, skill, character, and diligence, and hence also for granting privilege.

Along with universal schooling, however, also came the obsession with using examinations as the exclusive measure for talent in the modern education system. This was a holdover from Confucianism, to be sure, but also the result of Japanese influence in the first half of the twentieth century, when they ruled Korea as a colony. Thereafter Koreans came to recognize that this approach, while rewarding merit to a certain degree, was also patently unfair and not the best way to cultivate an open, just society, because such a system disadvantaged the poor and limited the life possibilities of most exam takers. It also robbed teenagers of valuable experiences in intellectual exploration, problem solving and citizenship, as they became absorbed in rote learning and exam preparation.

The reason why this fundamental problem, despite its widespread recognition, did not get solved was probably related to the reason why economic power, too, tended to become concentrated in South Korea. Elites who benefited from the openness of modern institutions, whether through the education system or the capitalist free market, protected or expanded their privileges by resorting to Confucian familism. Much of this was unavoidable. Who, after all, could dismiss the value of working hard and accumulating wealth for the sake of one's children and relatives? But when such practices become excessive by unfairly blocking others' access to privileges and resources, society eventually reverts to ancient patterns of exclusivity.

This risk has become most apparent in the realm of politics. South Koreans in the modern era can actually point to a lot of progress in this regard. Their political leaders, social activists, and elected representatives, including presidents, have come from a variety of socioeconomic and religious backgrounds. But as we know, the protection of privileges through inherited power and other closed methods have often prevailed, even after the democratization of the late twentieth century. The danger of such outcomes, which seems so contradictory to the ideals of a fair and democratic society, is widely perceived around the world, but South Koreans probably have less excuse for complacency: They were ruled by a monarchy just seventy years ago, under Japanese domination. Furthermore, they need only to look at their neighbors to the North for a picture of what happens when a closed Korean society is taken to its logical end.

Chapter 32

THE NORTH KOREAN VIEW OF HISTORY

In North Korea, history shapes just about everything. History refers here not only to the past, but also to people's historical views, or their interpretation of historical events and patterns. The orthodox North Korean perspective, the only one permitted, views most of Korean history as a series of struggles by the people. Internally, they fought cruel exploitation by the hereditary ruling elites and capitalists. The masses, including slaves, worked in the fields or engaged in other labor, but the fruits of their efforts were mostly stolen by the unproductive aristocrats, landlords and merchants. Government officials are also depicted as having squeezed the people by collecting burdensome taxes while offering few benefits in return. Skilled mostly in abstract and useless learning, such elites were too preoccupied with political intrigue to care for regular people or even to protect them from foreign invasions.

The magnitude of these external dangers is usually portrayed as threatening the very existence of the Korean nation. From the continent came attacks by the Chinese and by people of the northern Asian areas, stretching from Mongolia to Manchuria, who periodically controlled China. In the seventh century, the Chinese Sui dynasty tried to obliterate the ancient kingdom of Goguryeo, and the Tang dynasty tried to grab the Korean peninsula from the Silla kingdom. In the Goryeo era of Korean history, various north Asian groups launched attacks, but the biggest force was the Mongols, who successfully conquered the country and ruled it indirectly for a century. Then in the Joseon era came the devastating Japanese invasions of the late sixteenth century, followed quickly by the Manchu invasions, and then the Japanese again in the early twentieth century.

To North Koreans, throughout this long experience of suffering at the hands of both internal and external forces, the brave and virtuous common people, armed with their unshakable sense of patriotism and propriety, persisted and often resisted. Furthermore, they were sometimes led by great figures who rallied the people and guided them toward actions that saved the country.

This role of the great salvational hero is what makes the North Korean view of history so important to understanding North Korea. A people-centered historical perspective itself is nothing new. It is a typically communist or nationalist historical interpretation, and in fact this version of pre-1945 history is remarkably similar to common views in South Korea. But the North Korean historical understanding, with its central role for the visionary leader, is also a setup. It is a retroactive fabrication.

Kim Il-Sung, the longtime ruler of North Korea from 1945 to 1994, is the reason why Korean history is interpreted as a progressive struggle against internal, and especially external, foes that required final deliverance by a great hero. Kim, it appears, was indeed a military commander in the 1930s, when Korea was under Japanese colonial rule. But he was among many leaders of guerrilla bands operating in China and Manchuria. In fact, his particular group was part of a larger effort organized by the Chinese communists against Japan. By the end of the decade, Kim went into hiding in the Soviet Union for the final stages of the Pacific War. When he returned to Korea soon after liberation in 1945, he was selected by the Russians, who occupied northern Korea, as their native communist leader.

From this privileged role, Kim was able to amass enough power to occupy a commanding position when North Korea was formally founded in 1948. With approval from the Soviets and the Chinese, he then launched the Korean War in June 1950. On the verge of defeat in late 1950, he was saved by the massive entry of Chinese troops on the Northern side. Kim worked to eliminate internal political rivals after the Korean War, which ended in a stalemate in 1953, but this was difficult because they were attached to the Soviets and the Chinese, the main sources of the military and financial aid for his regime. He also began to intensify the Orwellian invention of history in order to solidify his claims as a nationalist leader who successfully beat back both foreign invaders and foreign influence, whereby this indispensable Soviet and Chinese role in the creation and early survival of North Korea began to disappear from official memory. In other words, a history was crafted that baldly denied the reality of Kim's dependence on foreign forces.

This refashioned historical perspective in North Korea went far beyond embellishing Kim's exploits as an anti-Japanese guerrilla fighter. He was now credited with nothing less than liberating Korea from Japanese colonialism in 1945. He also claimed responsibility for defeating the Americans in the Korean War and hence for protecting the nation from foreign aggression, just like the Korean heroes of the past, but on a more glorious scale.

These fabrications and others remain at the heart of the approved North Korean understanding of history, and in turn they uphold the entire political and social structure of North Korea. In sum, the acceptance of Kim's descendants as the country's rightful leaders depends on the perceived legitimacy, based almost exclusively on invented history, of Kim Il-Sung himself.

Chapter 33

ANOTHER WAY TO VIEW NATIONAL DIVISION

For more than a generation, surveys have shown a weakening resolve among younger South Koreans to achieve reunification. Understandably, societal leaders and elders have perceived this development as deeply alarming, even scandalous. The diagnoses have ranged from excessive materialism and individualism to a general apathy about social or political matters, including ignorance of Korea's history. But a closer examination of Korean history also suggests that the concept of national division itself might be problematic.

Most Koreans today, in both North and South, have come to internalize the idea that Koreans make up an inviolable, indeed homogeneous ethnic nation, bound foremost by shared ancestry and culture. Korean schoolchildren are still taught that the Korean nation is about 5,000 years old and began with the mythical progenitor, Dangun. Though fundamentalist Christians and others have objected, most Koreans have come to accept this story as a kind of harmless legend that strengthens national identity and speaks to the inherent unity of the Korean people. They tend to perceive the current political division, therefore, as not only improper but unnatural.

Like religious identity, then, national identity seems almost inescapable, even though no one is born with any particular national gene. National identity is a social construct, or more accurately, a historical construct, and it is worth considering that the construction of Korean national identity has usually served political or other particular interests, and that Korean nationhood is a complicated matter, if history is any guide.

Over the past decade or so, for example, South Koreans have been compelled to reassess the criteria of their nationhood if they are to deal properly with the realities of immigration. Ancestry or "blood" cannot be the basis of Korean national identity anymore, because that would exclude an increasing number of residents who are recent immigrants or their descendants. Actually, throughout the verifiable length of Korean history (which, while not close to 5,000 years, is still very long), waves of immigrants, voluntarily and often otherwise, have settled in the peninsula. Koreans have hardly been a homogeneous people.

What of the notion that Koreans are identifiable through their unique culture and values? In terms of religion, this certainly is not true. In fact, religious and cultural diversity have been stalwart features of Korean history, which makes sense, given that political unity and social control have usually come through forceful means to serve elite, minority interests. This process began in the seventh century, when Silla, one of the so-called Three Kingdoms on the peninsula, conquered the other two, with the help of China. For this and other reasons, the notion of a "Silla unification" has come under assault. In fact, official histories in South Korea now claim that the ensuing two-century period was one of "the first north-south division," when Silla ruled the southern part of the peninsula, while a partially Korean kingdom, Balhae, ruled the north. If so, from the beginning Korean states contained multiple ethnicities.

Indeed, in terms of a shared geography, the whole of the Korean peninsula has been a unified territory for only the past 600 years or so. Relatively speaking, six centuries is a long time compared to most other nations, but it does not exactly suggest primal origins. And upon the founding of the Joseon kingdom in the late fourteenth century, the government undertook a massive settlement program to populate the northern one-quarter of the peninsula, which had not been part of the preceding Goryeo kingdom (918–1392). The government also sought to incorporate the Jurchen and other peoples living there into Joseon political rule.

What, then, of a unified language as a bedrock feature of Korean nationhood? While for the most part Korean dialects are mutually intelligible, there are plenty of languages around the world (English, Arabic, Spanish, Chinese, Dutch, French) that are shared by very distinctive countries and even separate ethnic groups. The common language of English is not strong enough to foster a meaningful sense of unity even among the countries in the British Commonwealth (such as India, Australia, New Zealand, South Africa and Canada), much less between places like the United States and Ireland. And some nationalities, like the Swiss, are perfectly fine with speaking several different languages. The point is that historical developments have rendered shared language often incapable of overcoming national and ethnic divisions, and that multiple languages do not necessarily prohibit a sense of common identity.

For the Korean case, one can argue that the most powerful historical factor to inspire unity has actually been a shared government, or a common experience of political rule, whether controlled by native groups or foreign occupiers. And these political forces, more than anything organically derived from social and cultural interaction, have effectively constructed national identities

and histories in order to achieve certain goals, such as the legitimacy or domination of a new political order.

It has been more than a century since Korea was last ruled by a single,
native governing entity. One suspects, then, that the continuing strength of
Koreans' sense of nationhood is more the result of strenuous, organized
efforts to overcome the long-term consequences of the 1910 Japanese conquest, and then of the North–South division installed in 1945, rather than to
restore some innate Korean unity.

Chapter 34

THE FIRST NATIONAL ASSEMBLY ELECTIONS

The first National Assembly election in South Korea took place in 1948, even before the Republic of Korea formally existed. In creating the first National Assembly, or the "Constitutional Assembly," that election laid the foundation for the South Korean state and political system. It was anything but a straight-forward process, however, and thus the complex legacy of that vote remains strong today.

The first major sticking point was that the 1948 election was limited to southern Korea, which was ruled by an American military administration, and held amid tremendous political and social conflict. After failing in 1947 to reach an accord with the Soviet Union to realize a unified governing system on the peninsula, the Americans kicked the "Korea problem" to the newly formed, and largely American-dominated, United Nations. The UN Temporary Commission on Korea could not gain cooperation from the Soviets, however, or even entry into northern Korea. It therefore proceeded, under American guidance, to set up elections in only the southern half of the country, to take place in early May 1948.

This sparked passionate opposition from a wide range of people, from communists to nationalists, who feared that such a step would harden national division. Two such figures, Gim Gu and Gim Gyu-sik, even took a trip to Pyongyang to meet with Kim Il-Sung, the North's communist leader. But upon their return to the south, they were condemned by the press for having been duped by the communists, which only helped the hardliners who wanted to move forward with the separate southern election. Needless to say, these two men, along with many other political and cultural leaders, refused to participate.

The most vehement resistance to the elections, however, came in early April 1948 from some inhabitants of Jeju Island who rose up against the oppressive actions of the police and right-wing youth groups, the most notorious of which originated in northern Korea. In response, these same paramilitary forces, along with army troops, terrorized the population and brutally killed thousands over the ensuing months. This was part of a general cleansing of leftist and even moderate elements who expressed opposition to the election and to the nascent southern system coming into form. Communist guerrillas throughout southern Korea continued their efforts to sabotage the election, but for the most part, they could not stop the vote, despite a variety of abuses and irregularities, including intimidation, bribery and fraud. While often having to wait in long lines, however, the people turned out in large numbers to cast their ballots on May 10, 1948.

Still, the main rightist political parties and organizations could not completely control the election, and their candidates were outnumbered by independents of various stripes, who won the majority of the Assembly seats. Despite the rightists' domination of the formal political system under American military rule, many of these figures had worked for the Japanese colonial regime, and this heightened the suspicions of those Koreans already wary of the potential descent toward permanent national division. The right wing was also split into two main factions, one that supported Syngman Rhee, the former independence activist who had spent most of his life in the United States, and another composed mostly of conservative landed elites and represented by the *Donga Ilbo* newspaper, headed by Gim Seong-su.

Upon convening on May 31, 1948, the Constitutional Assembly proceeded to select Rhee as its speaker. Rhee used this position to push through the two most consequential decisions by this body in drafting the founding constitution of South Korea. First, the constitution established a presidential system of government as opposed to a parliamentary one, a fateful move that would facilitate the concentration of power in strongmen over the course of the country's history, despite numerous calls to switch to a more democratic structure later. The single attempt at a parliamentary system came in 1960, but this experiment was quickly quashed by a military coup the following year.

Second, the Constitutional Assembly elected Syngman Rhee as the first president of the Republic of Korea, and both the president and the state were installed on the third anniversary of liberation, August 15, 1948. In hindsight, it became clear that Rhee had seen the first parliamentary elections and the Constitutional Assembly that resulted therefrom as part of a plan to seize authoritarian power. His ready disregard for the constitution's pronouncements of fundamental rights, including for workers and the political opposition, proved this again and again. As president, Rhee would exploit the inter-Korean rivalry and the Korean War to suppress dissent of all kinds in the name of anti-communism. To maintain support for this power play, Rhee had to sustain the country's dependence on the US military, on transplants from the North, and on pro-Japanese collaborators from the colonial era, almost all of whom held a fierce hostility to communism.

These maneuvers established the basic structure of social domination in South Korea thereafter. Little wonder, then, that historians have long expressed great regret about the manner by which the South Korean state came into being, starting with that first National Assembly election of May 1948. Those citizens who lined up to vote could hardly have foreseen such an outcome.

Chapter 35

WHO STARTED THE KOREAN WAR?

Figure 35.1 Memorial to the Korean War's Battle of White Horse Hill, Cheorwon, South Korea.

The war that used to be called "Yug-i-o," or "Six-two-five" (June 25) in South Korea is now mostly known, somewhat oddly, as the "Hanguk jeonjaeng," or "Korean War," even though "Hanguk" technically refers only to South Korea. This new standard term also seems to reflect the perspective of outside forces, although they were not really the main combatants and certainly not the main victims of this tragedy.

In North Korea, which insists that the Americans invaded the North that day in 1950, it is still called the "Fatherland Liberation War" (Joguk haebang jeonjaeng). It is clear, however, that the Korean War began when the North Korean army, under the direction of Kim Il-Sung, crossed the 38th Parallel border in a surprise attack before dawn on June 25, 1950. But we would do well to consider who else, beyond the North Koreans, contributed to sparking this catastrophic conflict:

The Soviets. The Soviet Union did not contribute troops to North Korea's invasion and publicly denied any involvement, but historical documents have revealed that the Soviet leader, Josef Stalin, gave the go-ahead and promised material and strategic assistance. The North Koreans could not have launched the war without Soviet permission, for the Soviet Union had as much to do with the formation of North Korea as anyone else. The Soviets entered the Korean peninsula even before Japan's formal surrender in World War II on August 15, 1945, and went on to exercise dominant control over their northern occupation zone. Most consequentially, the Soviet occupation installed Kim Il-Sung into his leadership position and suppressed all noncommunist political actors north of the 38th Parallel.

The Chinese. The Chinese provided a training ground for North Korean officers and soldiers who fought in the Chinese civil war of 1945–1949. Their return to North Korea before June 1950 would strengthen the North's readiness for the conflict. And China's leader Mao Zedong, like Stalin, had to sign off on Kim Il-Sung's plans to invade the South. It appears Mao was quite enthusiastic about the communists' prospects, providing assurances of Chinese assistance if necessary. This turned out to be a self-fulfilling prophecy, as the Chinese People's Liberation Army entered the war in late 1950 to save the North Korean forces and North Korea itself.

The Americans. Over the short term, the United States contributed to the outbreak of the war when then-Secretary of State Dean Acheson publicly specified, in early 1950, the areas of Asia that fell within the Americans' defense zone, a realm in which South Korea did not belong. This might have given a signal to Kim, Stalin and Mao that the United States would not come to South Korea's aid. They were wrong.

For as with the Soviet Union, the United States had invested too much in Korea to let it go, having entered as one of the two Allied occupying armies on the peninsula following Korea's liberation in 1945. In fact, the American State Department, hastily, had proposed the dividing line between the two occupations in the first place, and the United States had remained the foremost proponent of the idea that Korea needed superpower supervision before gaining autonomy. Like the Soviets, the Americans did not tolerate oppositional political elements in their respective occupation zone. This reinforced the division of the peninsula while assuring that a staunchly right-wing, anticommunist regime would gain power in southern Korea.

The Japanese. Of course, without Japanese colonial rule from 1910 to 1945, there would have been no need to "liberate" Korea and no basis for viewing Korea, as the Allies did, as an extension of Japan that thus warranted occupation.

South Koreans. After a long exile in the United States, Syngman Rhee had returned to Seoul by accompanying American General Douglas MacArthur in October 1945. Thereafter, even as the American occupation leaders grew weary and wary of him, Rhee maneuvered himself skillfully, and sometimes brutally, into a commanding position among right-wing political groups in Seoul (all others were prohibited).

Under Rhee's presidency, the Republic of Korea was formally inaugurated on the third anniversary of liberation, August 15, 1948. This South Korean state quickly eliminated the influence of moderate and left-wing elements, including desperate communist guerrillas scattered in the mountains. Rhee also began agitating and even planning for a military solution to national division through an invasion of the North. The North Koreans beat him to the starting line, but Rhee's actions might have accelerated this process.

All Koreans. As the opening months of the Korean War showed, there were also bitter social divisions in localities around the country that needed only a trigger to explode into horrific brutality. These divisions were expressed as class, familial and religious conflicts with origins that sometimes dated back to the nineteenth century. Such clashes had little to do with the geopolitical and ideological rivalries that set North Korea against South Korea and prompted the North to invade the South on that fateful day. But these hostilities surely contributed to the general atmosphere of strife and instability that led to what was, at its heart, a civil war, which perhaps is the most accurate label for the Korean War.

Chapter 36

TEXTBOOKS AND COMPETING
NATIONALIST HISTORIES

The bitter disputes in 2015 over whether the South Korean government should (re-)nationalize secondary history textbooks reflected stark ideological differences in historical understanding. But fundamentally, it was a struggle between two forms of Korean nationalism, and in turn between opposing visions of political legitimacy and modern identity.

The progressive (or "leftist") view is grounded in an ethnic Korean nationalism that sees modern history, dating back over a hundred years, as an upward path toward achieving an independent and united collectivity. Beginning in the late nineteenth century, Koreans undertook this march toward freedom and advancement but were quickly overcome by external forces, particularly Japanese imperialism, which forced Korea into a protectorate in 1905 and colonized the country in 1910. Ever since that period, Koreans have struggled not only to regain their autonomy but to create a more just society without political and economic exploitation. A return to the old days of a dynastic state and a hereditary social order was not sought, in other words; rather, a more enlightened, equalized and fair collectivity that freed itself from foreign domination would be the goal of the country's modern course of history.

From this view, then, what actually took place upon Korea's liberation in 1945, after thirty-five years of Japanese colonial rule, was indeed tragic. The superpower occupations divided the country and, in the south, those Koreans who had benefited from Japanese domination maintained their privileged social and economic standing. The period from 1945 to 1953, beginning with liberation and ending with the Korean War that solidified national division, thus represented another lost opportunity to achieve the nation's modern historical purpose.

Not to be defeated, however, the people continued thereafter to wage a struggle against oppressive forces: the regimes of Syngman Rhee (1948–1960), Park Chung-Hee (1961–1979) and Chun Doo-hwan (1980–1987), each of which began and sustained itself through violent, illegal and unjust means; the Cold War system, headed by the United States, which nurtured those dictatorships by prolonging national division and socioeconomic injustice; and the social and economic elite established through traitorous collusion with Japanese colonialism, American geopolitical interests and Korean strongmen.

Hence, from this progressive view of the nation's modern history, even the 1987 breakthrough to electoral democracy can be lamented as a false victory, for it resulted in the maintenance of this larger structure of inequality and geopolitical dependence, up to the present day. Moreover, this apparently "democratic" system has perpetuated national division, thereby preventing the achievement of the truly great goal of Korea's modern history.

The opposing conservative historical view, in a way, does not disagree on this final point: Democratization has indeed furthered the national divide, but South Koreans should be proud, not ashamed, of this reality. If the left-nationalist perspective is firmly grounded in ethnic nationalism, in other words, the right-nationalist view is centered on South Korean nationalism, which sees Korea's division as a hurdle to overcome, but not at the expense of weakening a sense of accomplishment for at least the southern half of the peninsula. Public education, then, should be geared toward instilling pride in the extent to which South Korea, at least, has achieved a genuinely modern and free nation-state. Sure, there have been problems and painful sacrifices in achieving a thriving, prosperous liberal democracy, but this great goal has been attained, and so it was all worth it.

Such a triumphalist South Korean nationalism thus views the path of modern Korean history as having forked in 1945 or 1948, with half of the country, as it turned out, going in the correct direction. Hence the terrible episodes of mass violence, massacres, assassinations, coups, torture, and stifling corruption that marked this course in South Korea thereafter were regrettable, but they were counterbalanced by the tremendous feats under the same circumstances: the rise from poverty to economic plenitude through industrialization; the ability to fend off communization and the North Korean threat under a strong ethos of anticommunism; and the development of a middle-class and consumerist society that finally made possible the great breakthrough to democratization in 1987.

In fact, from this perspective, South Korea was not ready for democracy until the late 1980s because of its economic and geopolitical circumstances. Thus, democratization came only when the country was properly developed in more basic ways while under the protection of the American-led Cold War order. In hindsight, then, the entirety of South Korea's history, if not of modern Korean history as a whole, contributed to this great enterprise. In short, the ends justified the means.

Needless to say, such a sentiment is very convenient for those in power or positions of economic privilege, for it legitimates their standing. That only begins the problems with this glorified South Korean nationalist understanding of history, which is disturbingly simplistic, even childish, in trying to whitewash the uncomfortable facets of the country's history. To do so, it relies on a neat, holistic, self-enclosed framework of the nation's past that stands at odds with how history actually unfolds. But in this regard, the South Korean nationalist view also has a lot in common with the ethnic Korean nationalism of the left.

Chapter 37

THE COMPLEXITIES OF
MEMORIAL DAY

Figure 37.1 Gravesites in the National Cemetery (Hyeonchungwon), southern Seoul.

Like many other nations victimized by imperialism and colonialism, South Koreans have faced difficult decisions about the ways they remember their military history. The observance of Memorial Day (Hyeonchungil) in South Korea every June 6th, for example, normally honors independence fighters against Japanese rule or soldiers who died in the Korean War or Vietnam War, but not the tens of thousands of Koreans who fought in World War II, a glaring omission. Such dilemmas raise very important questions, however,

Figure 37.2 Memorial statue and fountain at the entrance to the National Cemetery.

about how to view modern Korean history as a whole. We can begin with why certain soldiers are commemorated, while others are not.

Those who served in the South Korean military during the Korean War included many, especially in the commanding ranks, who also served the Japanese empire in its wars of imperialist aggression throughout Asia. These men are understandably counted among the fallen heroes, but only by ignoring the fact that they had also fought, in effect, against Korean independence during the Pacific War of World War II.

What explains this contradiction? It is the same reason why the thousands of Korean soldiers who died in World War II are almost completely forgotten. Many of them "volunteered" for the Japanese army from 1938 to 1944, but it turns out that most of these volunteers were forced into this duty by poverty or other circumstances that had nothing to do with their allegiance to the Japanese empire. The rest of the Korean soldiers in the Pacific War were conscripted, even apprehended, into military service between 1944 and 1945. In other words, they, too, were victims of Japanese colonial rule. Shouldn't this make them worthy of commemoration today?

The problem is that distinguishing between the true volunteers who fought willingly for Japan, on the one hand, and those who were forced into these terrible circumstances, on the other, is simply not possible, given the existing documentary evidence. And even if this evidence were available, how could one make such judgments about who enlisted with "proper" motives and who did not?

So the larger problem is more ethical and philosophical. Should Memorial Day and other efforts to commemorate military duty recognize only those who fought in the "good" wars? The soldiers, though, like those who fought in World War II, did not have a say in whether their particular war was just or legitimate. Almost all of them fought because they were forced to do so by the political system in place at the time. This was true all over the world and throughout history.

In some cases, this issue is more clear-cut. Almost no one today, for example, would favor a memorial or holiday dedicated to honoring the German soldiers of World War II, given that Germany was the clear aggressor in that conflict and perpetrated the mass murder of civilians such as with the Holocaust. And while the parallels are not absolute, we cannot salute the Japanese soldiers in the imperial army that rampaged through Asia while committing genocide and other atrocities, even if they were not in positions of making battlefield decisions. As Japanese, they bear the responsibility, in some form or another, for the horrors inflicted on the peoples of Asia and the deaths of millions of (mostly Chinese) civilians.

But where does this leave the Korean soldiers in the Japanese army? Were they also contributors to Japan's imperialistic aggression? Or were they, as people who were colonized by Japan, also victims? The official judgment of the South Korean government appears to be that they were more the former than the latter. Otherwise, the Korean soldiers of World War II would be commemorated on Memorial Day, one would think. So this raises another disturbing question: Should nationalism remain the standard for judging the propriety of a war, and how should war itself be commemorated?

This issue is relevant also for considering South Korea's participation, on the American side, in the Vietnam War from the mid-1960s to the mid-1970s. Aside from the conscripts, many Korean soldiers who went to Vietnam did so knowing well the stakes, given the pervasive ideology of anticommunism. Still others volunteered for service seeking adventure or fortune. Regardless, like the Americans, South Korean soldiers in the Vietnam War committed atrocities on innocent civilians, a fact that began to be openly discussed in the 1990s with the onset of democratization. And it has long been well known that many South Korean soldiers, including those honored in national cemeteries and national holidays, engaged in mass killings of civilians during the Korean War.

One cannot account morally for these unsettling facts without facing perhaps the most uncomfortable question of all on Memorial Day: Why does South Korea—or any country, for that matter—commemorate fallen soldiers in the first place? If the purpose is to perpetuate a simplistic nationalist view of a very complex and disturbing history, then it seems to do a disservice to those who died in these battles. Short of memorializing all victims of war regardless of nationality, the only way to truly honor the fallen soldiers is to consider, thoughtfully and carefully, why and how these military conflicts occurred in the first place.

Chapter 38

ADOPTION'S SPOTLIGHT ON KOREAN HISTORY

The tragic 2017 suicide of a Korean-born adoptee from the United States prompted uncomfortable reflection in several ways, including on the history of "undesirable" Korean children. This was the term used by a doctoral student of mine who wrote her dissertation on Korean orphans, vagrant children, and others who came to be identified, educated and regulated in the modern era.

Societies have always had to account for children in such unfortunate circumstances, and most modern societies developed systematic ways to attend to them, a process usually led by the state. In cultivating people to become proper, loyal citizens, the modern state gradually institutionalized the methods of schooling and reforming undesirable children. Charities and religious orders also did their part, and authors and journalists played a key role in making such children visible to the larger public through media such as newspapers, films and novels. Classic works of literature, such as Charles Dickens's "Oliver Twist," featured the orphan, for example, as a metaphor for the disruptions of modern life.

In Korea as well, orphans have played an outsized role in mass culture that transcends their real numbers. This is particularly striking because the traditional Confucian family system seemed unable to treat orphans and other such children as normal members of society. Before the late nineteenth century, most of these children were expected to be taken in by relatives, even if they were distant, and the state appears to have offered few institutional means to take care of them. With the arrival of Western missionaries in the mid- to late nineteenth century, orphanages and special schools began to appear, which became models for Koreans in setting up their own institutions.

The modernizing state followed suit at the turn of the twentieth century by establishing government-run orphanages and reformatory schools. And in the Japanese colonial period beginning in 1910, the state pursued a more systematic approach that sought to intervene in the workings of private orphanages as well. Whether public or private, these institutions all sought the same thing: to take these children off the streets and place them in settings that would "correct" their life path toward that of good citizens. So there were dual impulses at work, according to my student's research: to save and rescue the children, but also to regulate and discipline them.

The problem was that, like in many other places around the world, the shame attached to family-less or otherwise undesirable children made it difficult to integrate them into regular society. In Korea, not just orphans but children of widows, unmarried mothers, and concubines also continued to carry stigmas held over from premodern times, and their positions might have worsened due to the Japanese promotion of the nuclear family, instead of the extended family, as the new norm. In the latter colonial era, including the wartime mobilization period of the 1940s, these undesirable children became unwitting symbols of the sufferings of Koreans as a whole: somewhat homeless and excluded in their own land under Japanese domination.

Such children, however, did not fare much better following liberation in 1945, despite the rise in public concern and accommodation. The devastation of the Korean War period, from the late 1940s to 1950s, dealt a further blow while introducing more complications. Most wars produce orphans, of course, but the Korean War orphans brought (back) another main actor into the equation: Americans. The United States's central role in the war produced the well-intentioned but problematic intervention of American charities such as adoption agencies. In fact, some of the most famous adoption agencies in the world today, including Holt International, emerged from the circumstances of the Korean War. Beginning in South Korea's recovery period in the 1950s, the Korean War orphan became literally the poster child for international aid efforts sponsored by the US government and adoption agencies. Their work in the 1960s accelerated greatly in taking undesirable Korean children to the land of South Korea's declared saviors.

Some of these children were mixed-raced offspring of unions between Korean women and American soldiers, but most were those of mothers and families who suffered from persistent social stigmas and government efforts to exclude them from the fold of regular society. Such circumstances, combined with the growing activities of the international adoption agencies, produced an extraordinary result: a systematic "export" industry in children that paralleled the export-led industrialization of South Korea.

The exporting of Korean children across the world over the past half-century, which continues to a certain extent, is a difficult, complex topic for almost everyone involved. For the children themselves, many of whom are now adults with their own children, the anxieties that face all adoptees are entangled with questions about how the geopolitical entanglements of South Korea's troubled history further complicated the picture. Adoptions thus shine a spotlight on broader developments in modern Korean history, including the persistence of traditional family values amid socioeconomic and cultural change, and the unforeseen impact of external forces.

Chapter 39

QUESTIONING MONUMENTS

Made of stone or metal, and often larger than life, monuments are meant to be permanent. The most celebrated ones are public memorials, built by governments and placed in communal spaces such as parks or in front of courthouses, presidential mansions, or other official buildings. Indeed the most massive, elaborate, or decorative government buildings act as monuments themselves.

This should not mean, however, that monuments are held as eternally sacred symbols. They reflect the particular historical circumstances of their creation, and their meanings can change over time. In the United States, this theme has come to the forefront amid ongoing, passionate conflicts over the dozens of statues honoring the Confederate States of America, the name for those territories that seceded from the United States to start the American Civil War in 1861.

Although a shocking number of Americans still refuse to acknowledge it, their civil war was undeniably fought over slavery. Those who insist that the war was actually fought over "states' rights" and the southern way of life seem to miss the point that what the Confederacy defended was the states' rights to keep and even expand slavery, which formed the basis of the South's way of life. Therefore, today's indignant protectors of such statues are upholding none other than the heritage of white supremacy, racial segregation and forced labor, which cannot be separated from anything else that distinguished the southern lifestyle. In fact the Confederate leaders themselves said so, explicitly, to justify their rebellion back in the 1860s.

Today's defenders of Confederate symbols also seem unable to recognize that as time passes, societies and worldviews change with new information and understanding. Just as we no longer can accept slavery and racial discrimination, it is difficult to accept public memorials to ideas and people behind the violence of slave labor, ethnic cleansing and systematic rape. (If we are stuck, we can always apply the Hitler test: Could anyone justify keeping an old statue of the Nazi leader for the sake of historical preservation?)

So look for further battles to come, as concerned Americans challenge more monuments and statues, not only of those southern leaders who promoted slavery and discrimination, but even of older, iconic figures like Christopher Columbus, the Spanish seafarer whose voyage in 1492 changed the world. Over the past few centuries, so central did Columbus become to the mythology of the Americas that his name became attached to just about everything: companies and institutions, schools and universities, a broadcasting network (CBS), and of course innumerable places. Indeed the US capital is named after him, as is an entire country in South America.

But historians have discovered something in documents such as eyewitness accounts, as well as his own diaries and reports: Columbus was not only a daring, if somewhat delusional, explorer, but also a murderous maniac, blithely killing or enslaving native Americans in pursuit of riches and in the name of his religion and monarch. And of course, his actions began the waves of genocide that killed countless millions of indigenous people from the sixteenth to nineteenth centuries, mostly through disease but also through targeted violence. Together with the transatlantic slave trade, another practice that Columbus initiated, this extermination of the western hemisphere's inhabitants made possible the European domination of the Americas.

One can accept this as simply the deeply disturbing reality of the past from which we can learn, and at least it's an improvement over the myths that were common until recently. But should we also simply accept the continuing display of statues, in public spaces, of people like Columbus? After all, these monuments honor not only a troubling historical figure but also past eras when such a man was ignorantly glorified.

Like many other nationalities in the modern world, South Koreans have become familiar with the sensitivities of such a problem. But they have mostly recognized that monuments, like laws and governments, are living things, originating in the past but continually refreshed with meaning as times and values change and understanding is gained.

Back in 1995, for example, some observers, including historians, opposed President Kim Young Sam's decision to take down the enormous building behind Seoul's Gwanghwamun Gate that had been erected, seventy years earlier, as the headquarters of the Japanese colonial government. Those who objected to Kim's decision argued that the building was distinctive, historically valuable, and reflected an undeniably important period in Korea's past, however unsettling. But this building was also constructed to serve as a monument to Japanese rule and all that came with it. Hence, despite its utility as a spacious structure that South Korean governments themselves had used for fifty years after liberation in 1945, its continued existence in such a prominent

Figure 39.1 Entrance to the Independence Hall museum complex, Cheonan, South Korea.

Figure 39.2 A display within Independence Hall.

public space, could no longer be endured in a new, democratic South Korea. In short, times had changed.

Removing outdated and inappropriate public memorials, in other words, is just as historically valid as keeping them in place. If they cannot be transferred to museums, then destruction seems unavoidable. This point might prove useful when the current North Korean regime falls, and all those huge monuments to the Kims and to "Juche" will likely be torn down. We do not know when this will happen, but it is difficult to imagine that Koreans liberated from totalitarian rule will accept calls to save these monuments in the name of historical preservation.

Chapter 40

TAKING OWNERSHIP OF THE PAST

It used to be said that unlike in most other democracies, in South Korea one's political identity depended on his or her opinion, ironically, of North Korea. Whether one was "conservative" or "liberal," or something in between or beyond, reflected mostly one's stance regarding the North.

Of course, it was more complicated than this. The issues that shaped a South Korean citizen's political ideology and affiliation usually were numerous and worked in complex ways. Still, this somewhat conventional analysis seemed, at heart, correct. If so, it was easy to see where such a reality came from: the fierce state ideology of anti-communism during the decades of authoritarian rule.

The 2017 election of Moon Jae-in, however, raised further doubts about this picture of South Korean politics, because the presidential campaign took place amid high inter-Korean tensions, normally optimal electoral conditions for conservatives. As it turned out, one of the least anti-communist candidates won the presidency, and he did so convincingly. We could suggest that special circumstances—namely the process by which the previous president, Park Geun-hye, was removed from office—made this particular election an exception to the rule. That is, as long as national division stays in place, disagreements over North Korea will probably remain central to political alignment and behavior in South Korea.

I would argue, however, that the 2017 presidential election showed the rise of another major factor in South Koreans' political identity and ideology: history. More specifically, since the turn of the twenty-first century, one's historical identification with the recent past, or one's sense of "ownership" over the nation's history, has become just as important. In short, historical views determine political views, and vice versa.

There is a generational aspect to this phenomenon. During the mass candlelight demonstrations beginning in the fall of 2016, for example, many middle-aged citizens expressed publicly their sense of ownership over the country's history, specifically the struggle for democracy. This was the notion that they must protect the democracy that they, as students and young adults, had sacrificed so much to gain. As the historical builders of democracy, they had to be its primary defenders. At the turn of the twenty-first century, these members of the "democracy generation" had driven an earlier wave of presidential politics toward the progressive side. They had insisted on overturning the simplistic anti-communism of their parents and grandparents. In doing so, however, they also testified to the persistent strength of the North Korea issue, especially as events originating in the North made such concerns unavoidable.

After sensing a grave threat to South Korean democracy from the old-style politics of anti-communism under the Lee Myung-bak and Park Geun-hye presidencies of 2008–2016, however, members of this generation appeared to reassert their social power. Furthermore, as the teachers, professors and parents of adolescents and young adults, they seemed determined to transmit their sense of historical ownership over democracy to the younger generations. Indeed, this version of history has long become the orthodox view in South Korea.

Outside the classrooms and universities, however, the oldest generations still cling to historical views rooted in anti-North Korean anti-communism, the Cold War, and the story of South Korean economic development out of poverty. They still speak of absolute, existential dangers of "leftist" ideology, which they see as threatening their own sense of historical ownership over the achievement of economic development while resisting communism.

This makes the youngest generations the main target of competition in the so-called "history wars": the narrative of anti-communist development versus the narrative of democratization. Struggling with economic inequality and pressed with other things to worry about, younger South Korean adults, who lack the experience of living under dictatorship, have not always drawn the connections between their lives and their history lessons.

What's more, since the early twenty-first century, conservative intellectuals have fought back against what they believe is an overly liberal historical orthodoxy, which in turn had developed as a reaction against dictatorship. But to do so, conservatives had to move beyond the traditional glorification of the authoritarian past, which no longer seemed viable. So they promoted another conservative sense of historical ownership: that South Koreans must take pride in both economic growth and democratization, which, along with the successful resistance to communism, should be seen as part of a greater, triumphant story of the country's modern transformation.

This "New Right" intellectual movement remained anti-communist, but it also tried to legitimize just about everything in South Korea's past by claiming that it all contributed, in the end, to national growth: The Cold War dependence on the United States, the economic domination of the big conglomerate companies, the persistent inequalities, and even the suppression of people's freedoms and rights were not only justified, but in fact were necessary to South

Korea's eventual triumph. Not surprisingly, this neat view of history was attractive to conservative politicians, who further promoted it in their policies.

It remains to be seen how well this countering sense of historical ownership can compete against the now-dominant, progressive view. But undoubtedly the stakes are very high, because one's position in these history wars, perhaps even more than one's stance on North Korea, will help shape the political landscape going forward.

Part VII

HISTORY MAKERS

Chapter 41

DEMYTHOLOGIZING KING SEJONG THE GREAT

Hangul Day, on October 9, commemorates what is generally considered the nation's greatest cultural accomplishment, the Korean alphabet, and its most revered historical figure, King Sejong the Great, extolled as the epitome of the "sage king." The strength of this legend is understandable; King Sejong was indeed a great man, and Koreans are no different from most other nations today that mythologize their heralded leaders from the past. But to truly appreciate Sejong's historical significance, it seems wise to demythologize him and his achievements a bit.

We can begin with the alphabet itself. Koreans have come to believe that *hangul* is the most accomplished writing system ever devised, the consummate blend of art and science. It is indeed wonderfully precise and flexible, but its relative merits are difficult to assess. It perfectly captures the Korean language, to be sure, and it appears to do well in expressing a foreign language like Japanese. For conveying other languages such as Chinese or English, however, *hangul* seems not as well suited. This makes perfect sense, for King Sejong and his scholars were not interested in creating a universal alphabet, just one that would match well the Korean language. And they did.

What of the claim that the script (called Hunmin Jeongeum when it was promulgated in 1446) arose from only scientific principles, that it was autonomously created? This may be what the Korean documents suggest, but specialists have pointed out the following: In world history, alphabetical writing, like writing itself, tended to get easily transmitted because of its wondrous utility. And Korean elites of that era could not have been ignorant of other alphabetical scripts, such as the Mongol writing system, particularly during the period of Mongol domination in the thirteenth and fourteenth centuries. To acknowledge that the great king borrowed from other scripts in creating the Korean alphabet would not minimize his feat, but rather acknowledge his wisdom and learning. The same goes for his other achievements. Indeed, if we step away from the nation-centered perspective on King Sejong, we can gain a fuller understanding of his impact.

It is well known, for example, that King Sejong encouraged innovations in science and technology. Korean schoolchildren can recite the long list of impressive inventions that he fostered. They also know that the monarch developed the Hall of Worthies (Jiphyeonjeon) as a research center dedicated to scholarship and education. What is less emphasized is that this agency's primary objective was to study and propagate Confucianism. While the Hall of Worthies promoted the newly invented alphabet, its primary intellectual contributions came in compiling and publishing books on Confucian learning.

As he stated in the famous preamble introducing the alphabet, one of King Sejong's motives indeed was to increase literacy, and perhaps even to emphasize Korea's cultural distinctiveness. But he also saw the script as a device to spread Confucian teachings more easily. The alphabet was quickly combined with the most advanced printing technologies, such as movable metal type, to publish not only vernacular literature, but also manuals on Confucian morality. Such fervent advancement of Confucianism certainly cannot be considered an attachment to things "Chinese," but neither was it an assertion of Korean superiority or cultural autonomy. Moreover, while the alphabet became a valuable cultural device for the masses over the course of the Joseon dynasty, it hardly gave rise to a thriving popular literary culture, at least compared to the impact of vernacular writing in other parts of the world.

In fact, for most of the Joseon era, learned Koreans tended to ignore this great potential of the alphabet. Many believed that using the alphabet tempted Koreans to do what other "barbarians" in East Asia did, namely, to steer away from Confucian values by using a non-Chinese writing system. Such powerful opposing voices arose immediately after the script's invention, and even King Sejong's lofty standing could not win them over.

What proved perhaps more durable in the Joseon era was King Sejong's instrumental role in securing the new territories of the new kingdom, which corresponded more or less to Hamgyeong province. This area had not belonged to the preceding Goryeo kingdom, and with the Mongol retreat from Goryeo beginning in the late fourteenth century, the Korean government began to claim more of it. It was sparsely populated, however, and most of the people living there were not Koreans.

King Sejong did more than any other monarch to implement a massive settlement of this land, almost exclusively with lower-status people, even criminals, from the southern provinces. Many of them were forced to move there, and this helped to establish the northern provinces in general as a kind of backwater, at least from the perspective of the central elites, who discriminated against the north in a variety of ways.

Such were some of the less-than-heroic, albeit unintended, consequences of King Sejong's actions. This perspective does not diminish him but instead tries

Figure 41.1 Statue of Jang Yeong-sil, legendary inventor from the King Sejong era, Busan National University campus, Busan, South Korea.

to view him more realistically, which may actually heighten one's impression of him. In fact, it is astounding that he managed to do all this despite being the son and father of murderous monarchs (Kings Taejong and Sejo, respectively) who usurped the throne. Now that was truly a great accomplishment.

Chapter 42

MODERN LADY SHIN SAIMDANG

Shin Saimdang, a figure from the sixteenth century, has become a hot topic, even glamorized by a television historical drama in 2016 that reimagined her life and connected it, through the reliable evocation of reincarnation, to the present day. A slew of novels, children's books, and academic works has also fueled this popularity, as has undoubtedly the circulation of the 50,000-*won* banknote that bears her image. Leisure and entertainment culture, consumerism, and increasing wealth, in other words, have helped laid the basis for her meteoric rise, as if she were some *Hallyu* star.

She might as well be. The opening episodes of that television series suggested another example of modernizing, through popular reinvention, a female figure from the distant past. In this case, Lady Shin was refashioned into the opposite of what she was earlier embraced for: a filial and learned daughter and wife, and the wise mother of the great philosopher Yulgok. Those qualities did not disappear in this television drama, but the greater motive was to show her as a daring and ingenious artist who pursues her true passions in the face of societal and familial constraints. She became, in short, the idealized everywoman of South Korea today.

Such an exaggerated portrayal might be objectionable, but this had been going on for a while. Just a few years earlier, Empress Gi, the Korean-born wife of the Mongol emperor in the fourteenth century, was reconceived by television as a male-masquerading teenager who then turns into a fierce Korean nationalist. And back in 2009, Queen Seondeok, the first female monarch of the ancient Silla kingdom, underwent the Hallyu treatment and emerged as a cross-dressing, visionary, socialist unifier who juggled complex romantic feelings.

Not as far-fetched but just as creative was the historical drama that perhaps started it all, the "Jewel in the Palace" (Daejanggeum) television series of the early 2000s that became a megahit across Asia, especially in China, and starred the same actress who later played Lady Shin. This dramatized profile of a low court lady, whose wit, skill and perseverance takes her from menial cook to status as a royal physician, highlighted the glories of traditional cuisine, medicine, and values, to be sure. But clearly, the appeal of the main character, loosely based on a real historical figure from the sixteenth century, lay in her being both traditional and strikingly modern at the same time.

Given what has been taking place in South Korea in recent decades regarding women's rights and social standing, such trends in popular culture are understandable. Since the mid-1990s, sweeping legal and social reforms have liberated women from deeply entrenched inequalities, and likewise Korean women have swept into the upper echelons of modern life, including even politics. Indeed that a woman would eventually be elected president by 2012 was not that surprising. And attitudes have changed so dramatically that even when such powerful women were discovered to be engaging in corruption and abuse of power, they were publicly condemned for their transgressions as if they were men. This can be considered a sign of progress.

Still, other signs and concerns of sexism in the popular reaction to the Park Geun-hye/Choe Sun-sil scandal of 2016 seem to have lain just beneath the surface, and this might reflect the delicate balance between customary and contemporary expectations that seems to burden women disproportionately. In such a way, these television dramas can serve as reflections of a growing awareness of stubborn biases and unjust hardships. If purveyors of popular culture wish to continue cultivating a more healthful and forthright image of women, as well as other marginalized groups, through dramatizations of history, I might suggest some tweaks to the formula, based on the Shin Saimdang television series.

First, it would be helpful to present a more realistic depiction of the debilitations of the Joseon-era social hierarchy. Lady Shin, in fact, was an aristocratic woman who owned dozens of hereditary slaves, which we know about through surviving family documents. But this TV dramatization and many others continue to put forth "happy slaves" as light comic characters, which makes for a sad irony in featuring the protagonist's struggles with gender discrimination while ignoring other forms of bondage, including those perpetuated by the heroine.

Second, it would be refreshing to watch a dramatization of life in the old days that is absent of court politics, especially the monarchy. The Shin Saimdang television series was set in Gangneung, Lady Shin's hometown, which lies far away from Seoul, but her fictional love interest was a wayward prince and, as if on cue, the factional politics of the capital eventually plays a role in the storyline. The latter is not completely unrealistic, considering that Lady Shin's ancestors and family members did include some political figures, but one cannot shake the sense that, once again, we were seeing the trope of a woman finding validation through a connection to the monarchy.

Figure 42.1 Statue of Sin Saimdang, Ojukheon Museum, Gangneung, South Korea.

Such hackneyed portrayals of royalty and conniving court ladies actually highlight the uncomfortable reality that everything in the public realm these days can have unintended consequences, even an innocuous television series celebrating female accomplishment.

Chapter 43

FIVE POTENTIAL NATIONAL HEROES

The turbulence and turmoil of Korea's modern history and the accompanying divisions over historical understanding in South Korea, which have been fueled by the intensive changes brought forth by both (anti-communist) dictatorship and democratization, make finding agreeable national heroes a very difficult challenge. Nevertheless, there seem plenty of good candidates for this imaginary pantheon of exemplary figures. Here are five such persons from the Korean past, along with a consideration of their contemporaries with similar qualities:

Bak Je-ga (1750–1815)

As a sterling representative of the great scholar-officials of the "golden era" of the Joseon era, the late eighteenth century, Bak Je-ga seems to have done it all. A renowned writer, calligrapher and government official, Bak authored one of the most innovative works to call for reforming traditional Korean society, "On Northern Learning." This book epitomized the forward- and outward-looking orientation of a circle of outstanding thinkers of his time, including the scientist Hong Dae-yong, writer Bak Ji-won, philosopher Jeong Yag-yong and King Jeongjo. The latter two are arguably just as worthy for selection, but there are already enough monarchs and philosophers on the established lists of great figures.

Yu Gil-jun (1856–1914)

Perhaps the most influential of all the "enlightenment" activists in the late nineteenth century, Yu Gil-jun was also one of the first Koreans of the early modern era to travel beyond East Asia. In fact, he journeyed around the world and wrote about what he observed. He was also an influential, pioneering minister for the Gabo Reform governments of 1894–1895. He might be tainted by his sons' "pro-Japanese" actions in the colonial period, but it would be difficult to categorize Yu Gil-jun himself as such. (Yu declined a nobility

Figure 43.1 Yu Gil-jun (courtesy of *The Korea Times*).

Figure 43.2 An Chang-ho (*The Korea Times*).

Figure 43.3 Choe Yong-sin (*The Korea Times*).

Figure 43.4 Han Yong-un (*The Korea Times*).

title after Japan's annexation of Korea in 1910, which he opposed.) Closeness to Japan also disqualifies Yu's equally accomplished enlightenment contemporaries Gim Hong-jip, Gim Ok-gyun, and Bak Yeong-hyo.

An Chang-ho (1878–1938)

On the west coast of the United States, An Chang-ho is celebrated not only as one of the great patriots who fought for Korea's liberation from Japan, but also as one of the first Korean Americans. Before his exploits as an independence activist in various regions of northeast Asia, An worked tirelessly as an educator, establishing one of the "new learning" schools in his hometown of Pyongyang. Captured by the Japanese in the early 1930s for his nationalist activities, including as a leader of the Korean government in exile, he was effectively martyred. Contemporaries who also met this end while struggling for Korean autonomy and unity include Gim Gyu-sik and Yeo Un-hyeong, but, unlike An, they survived past the 1945 liberation and became entangled in the unavoidably messy politics of the postliberation period.

Choe Yong-sin (1909–1935)

Like An Chang-ho, Choe hailed from the northern part of Korea and was closely connected to the development of modern education. As a woman who overcame her impoverished background to gain schooling in the early twentieth century, Choe was an emblem of the power of education, especially Westernized education, to change lives. Moreover, as a dedicated community organizer, and driven by her Methodist faith to work on behalf of the common people in the countryside during the colonial period, she epitomized both the opportunities and limitations of her era. Although she died young (from overwork, it is claimed), she was immortalized as the heroine in a famous novel of the time.

Equally prominent female contemporaries included Na Hye-seok, whose life and public expressions broke social conventions even more dramatically, but perhaps too much so; Gim Hwallan (Helen Kim), who became notoriously pro-Japanese; and Yu Gwan-sun, who unlike Choe became glorified more for her death than for her life.

Han Yong-un (1879–1944)

Perhaps the most famous Buddhist figure in modern Korea, Han was a great author, social activist, and outspoken advocate of reform for his religion. His nationalist credentials are also impeccable, having stood as one of the thirty-three signers to the March First Declaration of Independence in 1919. All this makes him a great representative of the many challenges that Koreans faced in the first half of the twentieth century, and he seems to have overcome these challenges honorably.

Poets such as Gim Sowol, scribe of the most famous verse of modern Korea, and Jeong Ji-yong, who infused the Korean language with great beauty, were probably more accomplished, but they did not have Han's broader social impact. And as intellectuals who ventured into the social and political arena, Yi Gwang-su and Choe Nam-seon were probably more prominent, but their explicitly pro-Japanese stance in the late colonial period tainted them.

Indeed, many cultural, economic and political leaders had to make difficult choices as Korea passed through the turbulent periods of colonial subjugation, national division, civil war (the Korean War), military dictatorship, rapid industrialization and democratization over the past century. But this is why most of them probably will never qualify for entrance into the national pantheon, at least not as unsullied heroes enjoying a consensus popular judgment. We might wonder about the practical merits of a thought exercise such as this, but it compels consideration of a wide range of issues about remembering national history, and hence national identity as well.

Chapter 44

A PORTRAIT OF GREAT PAINTERS

Recently in South Korea there has been a revival of interest in the painter Lee Jung-seob (Yi Jung-seop), who died in the mid-1950s while destitute and suffering from psychological trauma. This suggests a classic case of an impoverished, despondent artist struggling to gain recognition because his craft was far ahead of its time.

In other ways, however, Lee's life and career well reflected his time, which was a particularly turbulent period in modern Korean history. When he was born in 1916, Korea had just fallen under Japanese colonial rule, and he reached his artistic maturity during the years of the Pacific War (World War II), the postliberation experience after 1945, and the Korean War. Lee's surviving paintings, which unfortunately appear to represent just a fraction of his total output, seem to portray vividly the fierce determination to survive and express the turmoil of his time.

Indeed, many of Korea's most celebrated painters serve as illuminating representatives of Korea's past. We can begin with Gim Hong-do and Shin Yun-bok, contemporaries in the late eighteenth century and creators of the most celebrated paintings from the Joseon era. Gim produced many masterful works, but the most cherished today are his genre paintings (*pungsokhwa*), depictions of people of various backgrounds going about their daily lives. These treasured works offer an inquisitive and sympathetic perspective on their human subjects, who are the focal points of the illustrations, with most of the surrounding background omitted. Shin's genre paintings, meanwhile, take a stylistically different approach, filling in the brilliant details of the natural surroundings and mostly featuring a narrower range of human subjects: aristocratic males and glamorous females, particularly *gisaeng* courtesans.

Although prized for their distinctive techniques, the works of both Gim and Shin demonstrate the sensitivities and sentiments of the artists' real-life circumstances. They were both court painters, professionals in the Office of Painting (Dohwaseo) from long-established lineages of technical officials, or *jungin*, whose members also filled government posts as interpreters, physicians, accountants, scientists and legal officials. In the late Joseon era, the *jungin* belonged to a kind of middle class, suffering social discrimination due to their lower hereditary status below the ruling aristocracy (*yangban*) but also better educated than the majority commoner population. This likely endowed them with the motivation, insight and experience necessary to produce such sensitive depictions of Korean society. This is probably also why these genre paintings are more prized today than these artists' official works produced for the court, and more compelling than those from aristocratic artists like Jeong Seon, whose best-known works are classic landscape paintings.

Jo Hui-ryong, of the nineteenth century, was another *jungin* artist, as well as a renowned poet and calligrapher. Although not one of the court painters himself, Jo moved in their circles, and although he did not produce genre paintings, Jo's social standing and sentiments likely were reflected in his revolutionary flourishes to traditional themes. His most accomplished creations are paintings of plum trees and flowers that colorfully burst forth in unconventional ways, as if he were defying the constraints imposed on him by Joseon society. Such a theme became highlighted in director Im Kwon-taek's film "Chihwason," which dramatized the struggles of the painter Jang Seung-eop as a symbol of the injustices and instabilities of the late nineteenth century.

The final acclaimed court painter, An Jung-sik, remained active well into the twentieth century. In fact, his best-known work dates from the early Japanese colonial period: "Spring Dawn in Baegak [Bugak] Mountain" (1915), a pair of portraits of the Gwanghwamun Gate and Gyeongbokgung Palace with the graceful peak looming behind them. These two paintings, especially the second one, can be read as An's sorrowful retrospective on Korea's passing, showing a contemplative nostalgia for the country's traditional seat of political power following the loss of sovereignty.

The circumstances of Japanese colonial rule, however, also helped nurture the first generation of modern Korean painters, most of whom studied in Japan. Among the best known are Go Hui-dong, a descendant of a prominent *jungin* family, and Na Hye-seok, likely from a family of late-Joseon hereditary clerks, who as a teenager went to study in Tokyo. Back home, Na became a prominent artist, author, essayist and radical champion of women's rights. One can detect this perspective in some of her illustrations as well, which were Western oil paintings but mostly of Korean subjects and themes.

More recently, another artist from the colonial period, Yi Kwae-dae, has gained recognition as perhaps the most skillful modern practitioner of figure paintings, from epic canvasses featuring dozens of people to several remarkable portraits. Contemporaneous with Lee Jung-seob but living until the mid-1960s (it is believed), his work was mostly unknown until recently because, like his friend Lee, Yi Kwae-dae was very much a product of Korea's tragic mid-twentieth-century history.

He chose to move to North Korea during the Korean War, and so under the dominant anti-communism of South Korea, his works were forbidden and mostly forgotten. Now that they have been rediscovered, Yi Kwae-dae's extraordinary paintings can be appreciated for illustrating such aspects of Korean history as much as for their inherent artistic merit.

Chapter 45

FOUR YOUNG MEN FROM 1884

Figure 45.1 The four leaders of the 1884 coup (from left): Bak Yeong-ho, Seo Gwang-beom, Seo Jae-pil, Gim Ok-gyun.

There is an extraordinary photograph dating from the mid-1880s of four dashing Korean men, who look poised, confident, and ready to do big things. In fact, they had just done a very big thing: They had violently overthrown their government in order to push through revolutionary change. Alas, they themselves were deposed after three days in power, forced to flee the country as state criminals.

This was the famed Gapsin Coup of December 1884, and that famous picture was taken in Japan, where they had found exile. That event and these men captured both the perils and promises of Korea at the dawn of a turbulent new era. What had brought these four gentlemen together was participation in the emerging enlightenment movement of the 1870s and 1880s. Under the guidance of teachers like Yu Hong-gi and Bak Gyu-su, they became convinced of the need for fundamental social reform and for learning from the outside world. Their sense of an urgent common mission sharpened as they grew more frustrated with the pace of government reform, until finally in desperation they decided to take drastic action.

Within a year after that fateful act and their shared experience of fleeing to safety, they would go their separate ways. Strikingly, however, the destinies of each of the four would symbolize a distinct but representative path for the country as a whole in this period.

As the head of this leadership group, Gim Ok-gyun was the best known. Having grown up in political circles and passing the state civil service exam, Gim was appointed to increasingly higher positions in the central government in the early 1880s. He also visited Japan in order to observe directly the rapid advances being made there. Back home, he hosted meetings of like-minded reformists in the self-proclaimed Enlightenment Party, and through this network he organized the Gapsin Coup. Upon taking power, however briefly, Gim spelled out a sweeping program of modern changes, including diplomatic independence from China, the elimination of hereditary classes, and the reorganization of government to eliminate corruption and waste.

In Japanese exile, Gim lived anxiously due to threats and demands from the Korean court for his extradition. After nearly a decade in Japan, he moved to Shanghai in 1894, where he was assassinated. Ironically, Gim died just a few months before the Gabo Reforms of the summer of 1894, which implemented many of the fundamental changes that he had long advocated.

Bak Yeong-hyo would live to see the implementation of the 1884 program in his homeland. He had been the most privileged of the four coup leaders, and hence he had the most to lose: Bak was actually a member of the royal family through marriage. But like Gim and the others, Bak was willing to risk his life and those of his family to realize his ideals. Unlike Gim Ok-gyun, Bak would live a long life, the latter part of which was spent as a prominent political and business figure in the colonial period. As an emblem of Korean collaboration with the Japanese occupation, he came to be reviled by many of his countrymen.

The third and fourth ringleaders of 1884, Seo Gwang-beom and his distant cousin Seo Jae-pil, joined Bak on a journey to San Francisco in 1885. While Bak would soon return to Japan, Seo Gwang-beom stayed in the United States, moving to the east coast and attending school. This was when he likely received news that his entire immediate family, including his father, a vice-cabinet minister, had been executed, a gruesome end met by the relatives of some other coup participants as well. He endured through this and other hardships while struggling to live in America, and then returned to Korea following the start of the Gabo Reforms in 1894 to attain formal rehabilitation and a series of high-ranking official posts. He went back to the United States as a Korean ambassador at the end of 1895 and died there from illness in 1897.

Like Seo Gwang-beom, Seo Jae-pil moved across the American continent to settle in the eastern United States. He, in fact, became the first Korean American by gaining American citizenship in the early 1890s. But he was Americanized in other ways as well, having attended university, earning a medical degree, converting to Protestantism, taking an English name (Philip Jaisohn), and even marrying an American woman. He also became one of the first American missionaries to Korea, to which he returned, like Seo Gwang-beom and Bak Yeong-hyo, when it became safe to do so after the Gabo Reforms began in 1894.

In order to promote Christianity, enlightenment, nationalism and mass education, in 1896 Seo Jae-pil founded the Independence Club and *The Independent*, the first modern newspaper in Korea. Both of these organizations would exert enormous influence over the rapid changes taking place in the country at the turn of the twentieth century. Seo Jae-pil moved back to the United States for good in 1898, and remarkably lived another half a century, all the while working to achieve Korean independence from Japanese domination. Fittingly, Seo Jae-pil got a chance to visit his liberated homeland in 1947 before passing away close to his 87th birthday in 1951.

Chapter 46

NA HYE-SEOK

I have often wondered when the South Korean film industry, with its high production values and keen marketing sense, will produce a movie about the artist Na Hye-seok (1896–1948), one of the most interesting people in modern Korean history.

If done faithfully, such a film could highlight both historically important and highly appealing themes: love, romance, family drama, sexual scandal, faith and betrayal, art, politics, nationhood and modern social change amidst an epic backdrop. These themes would be embodied in three main characters, each a major historical figure during the Japanese colonial period (1910–1945). They also formed a fascinating love triangle.

Na was a painter, poet, novelist, essayist, and one of the pioneers of Korean feminism, as she called for changes in society far ahead of her time. Born in Suwon, just south of Seoul, Na was raised in a family of means headed by a father who served as an official in the Korean government, then in the succeeding colonial government. He was, then, no anti-Japanese nationalist, and in fact he sent his daughter, in her teens, to study art in Japan.

In Tokyo, Na Hye-seok engaged in painting, writing and publishing while forming close ties to other Korean students spending their formative years in the land of Korea's colonial overlord. Upon her return to Korea at the end of the 1910s, she worked as a teacher and continued to hone her craft as an oil painter. Then, despite her time spent in Japan (or perhaps because of it), she participated in the March First Independence Movement of 1919. She was jailed for this, but eventually freed after a few months, and the lawyer hired by her family to represent her soon became her husband.

For this man, Gim U-yeong, Na would be his second wife. But like Na, he was not someone caught up in tradition. He courted her, and their "love marriage" stood out when most marriages were arranged. He even promised to let her keep painting and pursue an artistic career, which bore fruit when, two years after March First, her works were displayed in a special exhibition sponsored by the colonial authorities.

Figure 46.1 Na Hye-seok (courtesy of *The Korea Times*).

Gim would have gone down in history as an important figure even had he not married Na. From a family of hereditary clerks near Busan, he represented a major social phenomenon: Many Koreans who, like Gim, came from non-noble backgrounds of the late Joseon dynasty took advantage of rapid changes in the early twentieth century, especially in education, to rise to new heights in the new social order. In the 1920s, Gim was already a top official in colonial Korea, and eventually he became one of the highest ranking Koreans in the Japanese imperial government.

His connections and prominence allowed him and his wife to travel to Manchuria and, in the late 1920s, to America and Europe. In Paris, where Na stayed for nearly a year while studying painting, she got involved in a scandalous love affair with a man twenty years her senior, Choe Rin. As a leader of the native Korean religion of Cheondogyo, Choe had been one of the thirty-three signers of the March First Declaration of Independence, for which he too was incarcerated. Thereafter, he became one of the best known social activists of the 1920s.

By the time he met Na, however, Choe had begun to retreat from his pro-independence passions, and by the 1930s, he conspicuously turned into one of the pro-Japanese public figures calling for Koreans' assimilation into the Japanese nation. In this way, he came to represent a larger trend, one that remains painful for many Koreans to reflect upon today: A contributor to the formation of modern Korean identity and culture, Choe eventually succumbed to the pressures of colonial rule and betrayed the cause of Korean independence and nationhood.

For Na, however, Choe became the source not of national betrayal, but a personal one. Upon her return to Korea, her husband, stunned by the affair and probably even more by the public scandal that ensued, divorced her, which cost her custody of her children and hopes for a return to normal life.

True to form, however, Na did not passively accept this situation. In fact, she sued her former lover Choe for violating her chastity and abandoning her, and she demanded monetary compensation for the enormous losses she suffered because of their affair.

Her point, as she would later explain in a published "confession," was that Korean men, including her husband, faced no social condemnation or even shame for their sexual activities outside of marriage. Women, in other words, were subjected to a double standard. But Na was not offering this social criticism just because she suffered its consequences directly; she had been publicly airing such views throughout her adult life, writing repeatedly of the need to emancipate Korean females through education and opportunity. Shockingly, she even targeted basic family conventions, speaking frankly of the debilitating effects of marriage, pregnancy and even child-rearing.

What Na expressed a century ago, in other words, would be seen even today as provocatively forward. Perhaps she is still too far ahead of her time, and that is why a movie about her, which would otherwise be so appealing, has not been made.

Chapter 47

HYUNDAI MOTORS AND CHUNG JU-YUNG

Hyundai Motor Company, one of the world's top automakers and, along with Samsung Electronics, the most recognized Korean brand on the global stage, has a history that well reflects that of modern Korea itself.

It begins with the founder, Chung Ju-yung, the legendary chairman of Hyundai. He was born in what is now North Korea in the early twentieth century, and by the time he passed away in March 2001, Hyundai had become one of the largest enterprises in the world and a symbol of South Korea's industrial might.

Hyundai Motor was established in 1967 as a favored component of Hyundai Corporation, which Chung had started in the early 1950s as a supplier and transporter for the Korean War. In the 1960s, Hyundai, particularly as a construction firm, grew hand-in-hand with the state-led development drive pursued by President Park Chung-Hee. Hyundai even built the Seoul-Busan Expressway, the main highway in South Korea, which opened in 1970.

The young car company, meanwhile, worked mostly on producing knockoffs of foreign models until 1976, when it introduced South Korea's first original car, the Pony. The Pony became not only a manufacturing milestone but a cultural landmark for the emerging urban, consumerist society. The domestic success of this model led to expansion into the international market, a process that achieved its first major breakthrough in 1986, when the Hyundai Excel began selling in the United States. There, the Excel became somewhat of a surprise hit due to its affordability, which was enough to tide the company over until it could improve the quality and technological sophistication of its cars.

Today, Hyundai Motor is much more associated with dependability than affordability, the result of an arduous half-century journey as the company became an emblem of South Korea's larger shifts in industrialization, digitization, and transformation into a postindustrial service economy.

But the company also became a site and symbol of major difficulties in the country as a whole. Due to its close association with the state, Hyundai's growth as a conglomerate and as a car company has always raised questions about the sacrifices made by its workers. This highlights, in turn, the broader issue of the extent to which famous tycoons, like Chung, should really be celebrated any more than the countless laborers who toiled in the assembly lines and struggled to make a living while contributing to the country's industrialization.

The suppression of workers' wages, rights and voices became a fundamental feature of this development story, backed by state security forces that violently stopped labor actions and arrested their leaders. The resulting, accumulating conflict exploded into full force the year after the Excel's heralded entrance into the US car market, as South Korea finally achieved electoral democracy in June 1987. This breakthrough in turn helped launch a wave of labor organizing and resistance throughout that summer.

One of the major results of these developments was the legal formation of factory labor unions such as that for Hyundai Motors, which assured that Hyundai's workers could now be represented collectively in their efforts to achieve fairer pay and safer workplaces. Such struggles continue to this day, but the notable improvements in working conditions for Hyundai employees since the 1980s were undoubtedly connected also to the higher quality and reputation of the cars that they built.

The other notable connection to larger developments, particularly in politics, came from the actions of Chung Ju-yung himself. Over his lifespan, Korea passed from the colonial period of Chung's birth and upbringing to national division, and then to the extraordinary rise of South Korea from the ashes of the Korean War to status as one of the world's largest and most advanced economies.

Although his company was largely a largely a creature (and vehicle) of authoritarian rule in South Korea, Chung showed a fierce will to take advantage of the democratic transition, as he ran for president in 1992 and garnered 15 percent of the vote. His entrance into politics, furthermore, was not driven merely by personal ambition; as it turned out, he was most interested in doing what he could, supported by the enormous wealth and power that he accumulated through Hyundai, to overcome national division. Despite his shortcomings as a political candidate, in the 1990s Chung played a key role in increasing interaction and reconciliation between the two Koreas. Indeed in 1998, as a gesture of goodwill for the starving people of North Korea, he donated 500 head of cattle to the North, ceremoniously driving them across the DMZ border—on top of Hyundai trucks, of course.

By then, Chung was in his 80s, devoting the final chapter of his long, colorful life to national reconciliation. Chung partook in the high point of inter-Korean relations since the Korean War by helping to arrange—through illicit donations to the Northern regime, as it turned out—the breakthrough summit meeting between the North and South Korean political leaders in June 2000. One is inclined to believe that this allowed him, in some measure, to die in peace the following year.

Chapter 48

YUN ISANG AND THE EAST BERLIN CASE

A deep sadness spread around the world in July 2017 with the death of Liu Xiaobo, the longtime Chinese dissident who had been incarcerated since 2008, when he helped draft an online statement calling for basic democratic reforms. He was widely admired for his courage in the face of oppression and in 2009 was awarded the Nobel Peace Prize, which he was not allowed to accept in person.

In fact, the Chinese authorities immediately condemned the Norwegian government, as if it could somehow revoke a decision made by the Nobel committee, and pressured foreign governments not to publicly support Liu as he rotted away in jail. Even after he was given a medical parole for terminal cancer a month before his death, very few officials in established democracies dared call for a complete release for his final days, and likewise world leaders mostly stayed silent after his death.

Such circumstances invite comparisons to the plight of a Korean intellectual, the noted composer Yun Isang, from over a half-century ago. In the summer of 1967, Yun, along with the poet Cheon Sang-byeong, painter Yi Eung-no, and scores of other innocent people, was jailed, tortured, and forced into confessions of communist subversion in what became known as the East Berlin Case.

Yun had been one of several Korean students in Western Europe at the time who took advantage of their relative freedom of movement and association by interacting with North Koreans stationed in East Berlin. The North Koreans of course had an interest in using these occasions to spread propaganda, and Yun even accepted an invitation to visit North Korea in 1963. He saw this as an opportunity to see some of the celebrated Goguryeo wall paintings that could inspire his music, a blend of Korean and Western conventions.

The East Berlin Case was triggered in May 1967 when another such visitor, Im Seok-jin, turned himself in directly to the South Korean president, Park Chung-Hee (who had just been reelected), and revealed details of the relationships centered in the North Korean embassy in East Berlin. The sensationalistic incident that exploded two months later showed well South Korea's ongoing descent into authoritarian rule. That dictatorship, however, would not arrive in full form until the 1970s, and this might explain why Yun did not suffer the same fate as Liu Xiaobo. Most important, perhaps, was the role of international actors, whose influence appears to have been far greater with the South Korean government at the time than with today's Chinese government.

This was because, incredibly, Park's security forces had reached into sovereign foreign countries, notably France and West Germany, to nab dozens of expatriate Koreans through deception, coercion, or outright kidnapping (though the current Chinese government has done something similar). They were among approximately two hundred people rounded up in July 1967 for even the slightest connection to the situation in Germany. Even with the mechanisms of an autocratic state working against them, however, the lack of evidence led to the early dismissal of charges against most defendants, although several, including Yun, were convicted and given harsh sentences. But the violation of state sovereignty in the South Korean government's kidnappings, as well as the violation of core principles of justice, brought forth a public outcry and pressure from the West German government, civic organizations in Europe, and renowned artists around the world.

It is difficult to determine which of those interventions played a greater role in convincing Park to change his mind, but eventually every single one of the arrested Koreans was released, including Yun Isang, who in 1969 was granted a "pardon" but forced to leave the country.

South Korean history is scarred with many such episodes from the dictatorship era, and some, including the East Berlin Case, were formally investigated after democratization in 1987. According to the government's exhaustive 2006 report, the entire affair, while sparked by Im's "confession," was concocted by the notorious Korean Central Intelligence Agency in the frenzy of anti-communism. None of the South Koreans arrested was actually guilty of spying, subversion, or even North Korean sympathies. Those who had taken trips to North Korea harbored no political motivation beyond curiosity and nationalist idealism.

Documents also showed that the Park regime pursued its case very publicly in order to intimidate into silence the growing protests, led by students, against the irregularities of the parliamentary election of June 1967. The apparent victories that Park's party won in this election provided enough seats to pass a referendum, two years later, to amend the constitution to allow Park to run for a third consecutive presidential term. All of this, in short, was part of a process toward implanting firmer dictatorial rule. In this sense, despite the differences with the Liu Xiaobo case, the larger commonalities are just as important.

Because he refused to accept the original verdict that had branded him a spy, Yun Isang, who was born in the 1910s on the south-central coast, never stepped foot again in South Korea before his death in 1995. He was buried in Berlin, and in 2017, South Korea's first lady, a former music student, visited Yun's grave to offer her respects, though no official expression of remorse. We will have to wait for this formal apology, just as we will have to see whether China will ever undergo the fundamental changes for which Liu Xiaobo had fought and died.

Chapter 49

RI YOUNG-HEE, ICONOCLAST FOR DEMOCRACY

The journalist Ri Young-hee (Yi Yeong-hui), one of the most influential intellectuals of recent times, helped shape the ideals of a democratic, and democratizing, South Korea. Even in the darkest period of the military dictatorship in the 1970s, Ri insisted on exposing the hidden causes of social inequality and national division, and on pursuing the goals of government accountability, press freedom and historical justice.

Ri Young-hee was born in 1929 in what is now North Korea, close to the Chinese border, and attended school during the wartime mobilization in the early 1940s under Japanese colonial rule. In his late teens and early 20s, after having fled the North, he witnessed the turmoil of the immediate postliberation period (1945–1950) under the American occupation and the early South Korean state. Following the outbreak of the Korean War in 1950, Ri served as a low-ranking officer, and in this position, he witnessed the horrific violence of the war, but also the brutality, corruption and abuses of the South Korean military. He found that many in the commanding ranks of the army were graduates of the Japanese imperial forces that had trampled over Asia during World War II. By contrast, at the bottom end of the ROK military, he found masses of mostly poor, undereducated and untrained young conscripts who were being used as cannon fodder. In the meantime, Ri's teenaged brother died of a ruptured appendix while caring for their parents in his absence. Ri later recalled that this mix of savagery and horror, as well as his guilt over his brother's death, was the turning point in his life and perspective.

After the armistice in 1953, Ri had to remain in the army and worked as an English language interpreter, a post that allowed him to observe closely the workings of his country's relationship with the United States. Upon his discharge in 1956, he successfully applied for a reporter's position with the Hapdong Tongsin wire service, through which he took his first trip to the United States at the end of the 1950s to study journalism at Northwestern University.

Figure 49.1 Ri Young-hee (courtesy of *The Korea Times*).

In his formative years, then, he experienced the dual expressions of American power: on the one hand, its overwhelming impact on the global order as an imperializing force in the Cold War, and on the other, its worldwide standing as the model for intellectual and press freedom. Such an ambivalent perspective on the United States would frame Ri's analysis of the relationship between Korea's internal and external conditions, and between its historical and contemporary circumstances. To him, national division and dictatorship could not be explained without a careful examination of the peninsula's place in the Cold War system. From his position as a journalist and public intellectual, Ri would devote his professional career to revealing and interpreting the intricate connections between these grand forces.

In the early 1970s, Ri was dismissed from his newspaper jobs as reporter and editor due to his published criticism of the Park Chung-Hee government. In 1971, he took a professorship in the Communications School of Hanyang University, where he established the country's sole research center dedicated to communist China. It was no accident, then, that Ri held a particular interest in the confrontations between imperialism and national liberation movements, including those in his home country.

Ri's public influence reached its peak during the trying years of the "Yushin" period of 1972–1979 when South Korea fell under an absolutist military dictatorship. His reputation for brave, defiant opposition to the regime stemmed from two collections of essays he published in the 1970s: "The Logic of Our Changing Times" (1974) and "Idolatry and Reason" (1977). The first book critiqued the Park regime's domineering ideology of anti-communism in the context of the Cold War, the Vietnam War, and the emergence of the People's

Republic of China on the world stage. This book became somewhat of a sensation in intellectual and student circles, and eventually Ri was forced off his teaching post at Hanyang University.

"Idolatry and Reason," published three years later, extended these points while more explicitly connecting the larger structures of oppression and inequality in contemporary South Korea to its troubled history. Ri insisted that the failure of South Korea to decolonize, or to remove the remnants of its colonial past, was most responsible for its internal repression and external dependence on the American-dominated security system of East Asia. For expressing such thoughts, Ri was quickly convicted of violating the Anti-Communist Law and jailed. His incarceration elicited public campaigns on his behalf from intellectuals both at home and abroad, and his release came in 1980, the year following the end of the Yushin system but not of military dictatorship itself.

Soon after South Korean democratization in 1987, Ri joined the editorial board of the newly established *Hankyoreh Sinmun* newspaper. This allowed him to openly promote those causes for which he had always worked passionately: press freedom, social justice and progressive nationalism. Ri continued to write prolifically until his death in December 2010, producing numerous volumes and remaining active in the left wing of the South Korean civic and intellectual realms. His legacy remains one of intellectual depth and integrity amid hardship, and of iconoclastic courage in the face of convention.

Chapter 50

KIM YOUNG SAM'S BROAD HISTORICAL APPEAL

Former South Korean president Kim Young Sam's death in November 2015 prompted much thinking about the historical significance of this man. Perhaps the greatest testimony to his impact came from the wide disparity of voices in the public realm that mourned his death. Prominent people and groups across the political and ideological spectrum claimed him as one of their own, as someone who had exerted profound influence on their particular group's perspectives and interests.

This may have much to do with Kim's very long political career, which began in the early 1950s and continued past his presidency of 1993–1998. More specifically, that both of South Korea's main political parties, in an age when the ideological rivalry between them was so bitter, could publicly revere him stemmed from his long-standing leadership in the fight for democracy. But equally important was Kim's decision in 1990 to "switch sides" and join the conservative forces for political expediency. This gave the conservative camp, up to this day, reason to proclaim themselves rightful heirs to the drive for democracy. In sum, the competing historical views that frame much of politics in contemporary South Korea accounted substantially for the outpouring of praise for Kim Young Sam across the political divides.

To progressives, Kim's decision to literally join hands with President Roh Tae-woo and Kim Jong-pil, the two most visible holdovers from the era of military dictatorship, in forming a large, coalitional ruling party constituted nothing short of a betrayal to the democratic cause. Since the 1970s, in political circles this struggle had featured the "Two Kims," Kim Young Sam and Kim Dae Jung, as part of a much broader anti-dictatorship movement that included the economic, cultural and religious realms.

It was perhaps his rivalry with the other Kim that led Kim Young Sam to conclude that joining the conservative camp in 1990, a move that he once described cryptically as "entering the tiger's lair to catch the tiger," as his best chance to win the presidency. And despite the sharp backlash from his former allies in the democracy camp, Kim probably felt secure in his identity and legacy. He had, after all, stood at the forefront of the resistance to the *Yushin* dictatorship of Park Chung-Hee in the 1970s. As the leader of the besieged opposition party, he had courageously and very publicly condemned the Park regime's excesses.

Kim's interview in 1979 with a foreign news outlet, in which he explicitly spelled out such abuses, got him expelled from the National Assembly. The immediate reaction to this move, by both fellow politicians and, more explosively, students in Kim's home region of the southeastern coast, led to Park's assassination at the hands of the Korean Central Intelligence Agency (KCIA) chief on October 26, 1979. When, contrary to nearly everyone's expectations, this extraordinary event did not lead to democratization but rather the opposite, Kim Young Sam continued to press for liberalization, even launching a hunger strike.

Alas, risking his life for the cause was not enough to gain the reward of winning the presidential election of 1987 following the democratic transition, for he had split the opposition's vote with Kim Dae Jung. And one cannot help but wonder whether Kim Young Sam became thereafter more determined to differentiate himself from the other Kim, and that this led him to take the fateful step of joining the ranks of conservatives in 1990.

After winning the presidency in 1992, however, Kim Young Sam did not retreat from his core, lifelong mission. Soon after taking office in 1993, he pushed through several reforms that secured South Korea's transition to democracy. These included the prohibition on using false names for financial transactions, a favorite tool for corruption; the formal recognition of the legitimacy of the Gwangju Uprising of 1980; and the dissolution of the Hanahoe group, a shadowy redoubt since the 1960s for military figures wanting to intervene in politics. These steps were followed by the prosecution of Chun Doohwan and Roh Tae-woo for their military coup in December of 1979, their responsibility for the massacre in Gwangju, and their astronomical presidential slush funds.

It was most of all these moves by Kim as president that conservatives today now hail as proof that democratization, coupled with the focus on industrialization, was as much a conservative legacy as a progressive one. After all, who today could praise the dictatorships of the 1970s and 1980s? Conservatives, then, can point to Kim Young Sam as the leading example of how one's experience in the struggle for democracy could naturally lead to a non-liberal political position. Many conservative politicians today, in fact, come from such a background, and to some of them, Kim Young Sam is their model and mentor.

To progressives, on the other hand, Kim's heroics lay in his pre-1990 actions, and his presidency's later descent into petty corruption, sense of malaise, and finally the economic crisis of 1997 was a truer reflection of his "turn." But even liberals have come to realize that, despite his shortcomings, Kim's contributions to the great epic of South Korean history were indeed monumental.

Chapter 51

KIM DAE JUNG'S HISTORIC ELECTION

On December 18, 1997, Kim Dae Jung was elected president of South Korea, leading to the country's first-ever peaceful transfer of power to the opposition. That alone would make this a momentous event, but the election's historical significance was even greater.

First, Kim Dae Jung's electoral victory represented the culmination of a long political career, most of which was spent in opposition to the South Korean ruling system. He helped lead the charge for democratization, and short of being killed, no one in the democracy movement suffered more than Kim Dae Jung. In the 1970s and 1980s, his life followed a repeated cycle of resistance, incarceration, hardship and freedom.

In 1973, after having come close to defeating Park Chung-Hee in the 1971 presidential election despite the many disadvantages he faced, Kim was kidnapped and tortured, and came within a few meters and minutes of losing his life. In an extraordinary turn of events, however, foreign pressure on the Park dictatorship intervened to save him. He spent the rest of that decade, however, more or less in domestic exile, under surveillance and the constant threat of more brutal government action against him.

In 1980, a few months after winning his freedom following Park's assassination, the ensuing military dictatorship of Chun Doo-hwan blamed Kim for arousing mass opposition protests, arrested him, and even sentenced him to death. His life again was spared thanks to foreign intervention--even from the pope, as Kim was a devout Catholic. And once again, he was sent into exile, this time abroad to the United States.

His return to his homeland in the mid-1980s helped charge the intensifying democratization movement, and after the 1987 breakthrough, it appeared that finally Kim would get a fair shot at becoming the country's political leader. This was not to be, however. Not only did Kim lose the 1987 election, he lost again in 1992, both times to the ruling party's candidate. So his victory in 1997, in his fourth attempt as an opposition candidate on the presidential ballot, came at the end of a decades-long journey to (peacefully) gain power. It was, in a way, the reward for dogged determination and undeterred ambition.

For his supporters, Kim's electoral victory thus constituted heavenly justice after a long personal struggle that had crippled him physically and scarred him psychologically. As the counterpart, in a sense, to Park Chung-Hee in the grand narrative of South Korean history, Kim Dae Jung was touted as the representative of an alternative path to modernization. His vision valued economic development, to be sure, but also human development, the prioritization of human rights and dignity over political and military strength.

To many others, this vision appeared naive and even dangerous, and his opponents repeatedly raised alarms about his prospective presidency by resorting to the age-old accusation of communist sympathies. But somewhat surprisingly, in December 1997 this ploy did not work, despite (or perhaps because of) the economic emergency that South Korea was experiencing at the time. Kim proved anything but a communist sympathizer or a severe partisan waiting to take vengeance against those who had oppressed him. In a gesture of solidarity and reconciliation in the face of the national economic crisis, among his first acts upon taking office in early 1998 was to pardon the same military dictators who had moved to kill him.

In hindsight, this appears to have been a mistake, but it again demonstrated that Kim Dae Jung was as much a pragmatist as an idealist. Under his leadership, the government repaid the 1997 IMF bailout loan ahead of schedule, and South Korea entered the new millennium in the throes of a very difficult economic recovery, which nevertheless attested to the power of concerted action. The country may have come together because of the singular set of urgent circumstances at the time, but Kim Dae Jung's leadership also helped.

And if nothing else, Kim Dae Jung's election and presidency, and indeed much of his life, shifted the center of presidential politics, however temporarily, away from the Gyeongsang region. Since the era of Park Chung-Hee every South Korean president, even of different ideologies and political affiliations, has come from that region, except Kim Dae Jung. Kim, from Jeolla province, offered an alternative voice in tackling the country's many divisions.

This takes us to the final point of significance of Kim Dae Jung's 1997 ascension to power. It represented a rare point in South Korean politics when a truly different approach to national division could be attempted. Kim Dae Jung's "Sunshine Policy" of bold, affirmative and steady engagement with North Korea, despite all of the compromises that this entailed, applied the basic principles that had driven his striving for democracy to an even greater challenge. And over the long term, the spirit of the Sunshine Policy, if not necessarily its specific steps, promises to be more productive and realistic than fearful hostility. This would also reinforce the wisdom of Kim Dae Jung's approach to governing as a whole, the legacy of which became cemented in that election of 1997.

Part VIII

EXTERNAL PRESENCES

Chapter 52

KOREA'S COMPLICATED RELATIONSHIP WITH CHINA

Ongoing attempts by the People's Republic of China to smoothen relations with both South and North Korea remind us how complex and problematic these ties have been over the past several decades. But this relationship between the peninsula and the mainland extends back nearly two millennia, to an era when the modern notions of "China" and especially "Korea" did not necessarily apply.

Since then, Korea's relationship with China has been one of "love–hate," oscillating from close alliance and peaceful cultural exchange to confrontation and bitter rivalry. Indeed, that Korea is still in existence is somewhat of a miracle, given the pressures that eventually extinguished the independent standing of most other smaller civilizations on China's periphery. But this survival, so central to Koreans' sense of national identity, also depended at times on Chinese assistance, which reinforces the difficulty of passing judgment on China's historical impact on the peninsula.

Without China, there might not have been a need for early polities on the peninsula to cohere into a single state. Korea itself formed, and continually developed thereafter, in opposition to China—a quest to distinguish the peninsula's people and governing order from that of the Middle Kingdom—as much as in emulation. Without question, since earliest times Korea's elites and rulers drew inspiration, models and other cultural features from China, the fount of high civilization. But Chinese attempts to conquer or absorb the peoples of the peninsula generated a fierce resistance that gave birth to Korea itself.

This happened twice in the seventh century, which can be considered the originating era of Korea as a nation-state, or at least as a distinctive civilization and coherent polity. Goguryeo, which began centuries earlier on territory that encompassed today's Manchuria and northern Korea, had to fend off waves of Chinese attempts to pacify and conquer it. The largest such campaign took place, it appears, in 612, by China's Sui dynasty.

Goguryeo successfully beat back the Chinese that time, but it had to endure several more such attacks, and finally it succumbed not to China but rather to an alliance between China and a peninsular rival, Silla. In the mid-seventh century, Silla finally brought resolution to centuries of confrontation between the peninsular states. It did so by turning to China, ruled by the Tang dynasty, for assistance in defeating first the kingdom of Baekje, on the southwestern part of the peninsula, and then Goguryeo. Almost immediately thereafter, however, Silla had to repel an effort by its erstwhile ally, the Tang, to absorb the entire peninsula.

Thereafter the dominant, though by no means exclusive, form of the Chinese–Korean relationship became settled: a tributary alliance in which the Korean state gained protection from its massive neighbor in exchange for ritual and material "tributes" or gifts that signaled a subordinate but still independent position. This worked in preventing the Chinese from taking further military action, but it did not always work in stopping other peoples who wanted to rule China from threatening and invading Korea. During the Goryeo dynasty (935–1392), which succeeded Silla, groups originating in Manchuria and central Asia, such as the Khitan and Jurchen, attacked Korea on its northern frontier. And finally the Mongols, on their way to conquering much of Eurasia, succeeded in subduing Korea. For nearly a century, Mongol-controlled China treated Goryeo somewhat like a colony, directly controlling its northern territories and constantly interfering in Goryeo's internal affairs. The Mongol emperor in Beijing even determined Goryeo's monarch, whose ancestry, beginning with his mother, was usually more Mongol than Korean.

The traditional relationship between China and Korea was restored in the second half of the fourteenth century following the overthrow of the Mongols by the Ming dynasty in China and the establishment of the Joseon dynasty in Korea. And further strengthened was China's role as the source of high civilization, as Joseon's founding fathers deemed a comprehensive form of Confucianism as Korea's state ideology, which included a formal reverence for China's superior diplomatic standing. This came in handy when Japan invaded Korea in the late sixteenth century. Without the Ming army's early and forceful intervention, Korea likely would have fallen, perhaps permanently, into status as Japanese territory. Of course, Chinese motives were not purely altruistic—they could not tolerate a hostile Japan on their border.

Such a realpolitik, practical view has always driven the China–Korea relationship, and China's last major intervention on the peninsula, too, should be remembered along these lines. When the new Chinese communist state aided the North Koreans in the Korean War in 1950, it did so out of its own interests, first and foremost. And it paid dearly, in the form of tens of thousands of Chinese soldiers killed in the fighting against the UN forces.

Since then, the communist alliance between mainland China and North Korea (and eventually the relationship between China and South Korea) has reflected the friendly as well as not-so-friendly ties that have marked relations since ancient times. Without Chinese support, North Korea would not have survived the Korean War and likely would not have survived the collapse of the Soviet Union in the early 1990s. Yet, in their official historical narrative, the North Koreans have denied this indispensable Chinese aid, adding another twist to China's multifaceted, complex role in the Korean past.

Chapter 53

HOW CHINESE WAS CHINESE HISTORY?

In the summer of 2017, Koreans became upset because it appeared that China's President Xi Jinping might have told his American counterpart that their country "was once part of China." But regardless of whether Xi actually said such an absurd thing, it's become apparent that the Chinese government, controlled by the Chinese Communist Party, has cultivated such a view to solve a fundamental problem with Chinese history itself. And the implications clearly extend to Korean history.

The common belief among Chinese, and many others, is that China boasts a long unbroken history as the Middle Kingdom that bestowed civilization to its neighbors while often ruling over them as well. But such a view is mostly just another modern nationalist myth, in this way similar to the idea that Korean history dates back five millennia.

Furthermore, much of Chinese history was not even Chinese. One of the fascinating features of "Chinese history" was that, throughout the cycles of dynastic rise and fall in political form, nearby peoples outside the kingdom's boundaries greatly influenced, and often controlled, the development of Chinese civilization. Following the primal, formative era, the earliest unified polity was the Qin dynasty of the third-century BCE, which militarily consolidated vast territories but quickly succumbed to the forces of what became the Han dynasty. Thereafter, for every "Chinese" dynastic order such as the Han, there was an extended period of fragmentation or rule by non-Chinese conquerors, such as the Khitan, Jurchen, Mongols and Manchus.

Even the famed Tang dynasty, which was contemporaneous with Korea's "Unified Silla" kingdom, was infused with a wide range of cultures, peoples and rulers, including from central Asia. Many of these smaller groups on the margins became absorbed into greater China, but others, such as those that formed what became Korea, were able to resist Chinese control, even as they were influenced by Chinese civilization. At the turn of the first millennium, the Han dynasty, which helped initiate the process of founding a coherent Chinese state, built scattered fortresses to anchor small colonies on parts of the Korean peninsula, but this was well before there was such a thing as Korea.

Just as important was that one of the native "barbarian" tribes on the peninsula whom the Chinese described so colorfully grew into a formidable kingdom and eventually overran the main Han outpost, located in what later became Pyongyang. This kingdom, Goguryeo, fiercely fought off Chinese attempts to invade and absorb it until Goguryeo itself fell to the joint forces of the Tang and another peninsular kingdom, Silla, in the seventh century. But when the Tang quickly tried to secure Chinese rule over the entire peninsula, Silla successfully repelled this effort. Thus was born the "tribute system" of ritual diplomatic relations, designed to keep the peace and Korea's autonomy, which more or less became the norm until the late nineteenth century.

So to use this ancient relationship as the basis for claiming that Korea was once a part of China is like stating that England was once a part of Italy, since the Roman Empire, which had similar outposts on what later became England, was geographically centered in territory that (much) later became Italy.

Or perhaps Mr. Xi was referring to the Yuan dynasty of the thirteenth and fourteenth centuries, when the Mongols conquered both China and Korea, and indeed much of Eurasia. But actually Mongol control over China was much more comprehensive and direct than over Korea, and in any case, it was not a matter of Korea being part of China.

Such interesting complexity in Chinese history reached a peak during the Qing empire of the seventeenth to twentieth centuries. This last Chinese dynasty was actually a product of the Manchus, offshoots of the Jurchen, who resisted the notion of assimilating with the majority Han Chinese, whom they had conquered after all. But ironically the commonly recognized, modern version of China resulted from this extended period of foreign rule: The Qing dynasty doubled the territory of the preceding Ming by absorbing the regions of Xinjiang, Tibet, Taiwan, and of course the Manchus' homeland of Manchuria. Little wonder, then, that even today the embrace of "China" among those living in these areas is somewhat questionable. Indeed, these people would identify much more with China's multinational history than with any sense of Chinese national history.

Since it established control in 1949, the Chinese Communist Party has in fact used this cosmopolitan past to promote the idea of a multicultural China of many ethnicities, including Koreans living in Manchuria today. Like the dynasties of the past, however, the Communist dynasty has manipulated history to legitimate and perpetuate its rule, and so, in a typical autocratic ploy, it has turned to stoking nationalism as well. In familiar service to strongman politics, then (see also Russia and Turkey), the Chinese government deploys both nationalism and imperialism, an "imperialist nationalism" if you will, based on a distorted glorification of the past. That seems to be the real story behind the diplomatic faux pas concerning Korea.

Chapter 54

TIANANMEN AND THE POWER
OF HISTORY

Three decades after the 1989 Tiananmen Square massacre of hundreds, perhaps thousands, of pro-democracy protesters in China's capital city, the citizens of China today remain forbidden from even mentioning this event. Courageous people in Hong Kong over the years have persisted in observing this anniversary, but they, too, are feeling increasing pressure from the authoritarian Chinese state. In an extraordinary violation of minimal global standards, Hong Kong publishers and journalists have even been kidnapped by mainland Chinese agents, including in foreign countries, for exercising their rights to free expression.

Why is the Chinese government so afraid? It has a lot to do with the power of history, and here we find some striking comparisons to what has happened in Korea, in both North and South, as well as in the East Asian region as a whole. The visit in 2016, for example, by US President Barack Obama to Hiroshima, the site of the first atomic bombing in August 1945, highlighted the major stakes of historical memory. Japanese Prime Minister Abe Shinzo used Obama's visit to reinforce Japan's victimhood, even as some of his own citizens condemned his ongoing attempts to recast history to minimize the impact of Japanese militarism in World War II. Abe, the grandson of a member of the warmongering cabinet of Tojo Hideki during the war, was pursuing an agenda of rewriting the postwar pacifist Japanese constitution through appeals to a skewed nationalist understanding of history.

The Chinese government's official response to the Obama visit, naturally, was to deploy the nationalism card and issue reminders of Japan's barbarous "Rape of Nanjing" in 1937. But the ruling Chinese Communist Party has itself manipulated and concealed history even more blatantly. The main problem is what to do with Mao Zedong, the founder of the party, the leader of mainland China from 1949 to his death in 1976, and the perpetrator of state actions that killed tens of millions of innocent Chinese people. While some terrible aspects of Mao's Cultural Revolution of 1966–1976 have been officially recognized, acknowledgment of the human cost of this insanity and of the Great Leap Forward in the late 1950s has been stifled. This is because an open accounting of this history would further jeopardize the legitimacy of the Communist Party itself. Such an official effort to cover up and fabricate history appears only to have intensified under the current Chinese leader, Xi Jinping.

The king of historical fabrication in order to sustain dictatorship was Kim Il-Sung, the leader of North Korea for half a century before his death in 1994. He actually copied Mao in instituting his own rule, but Kim went even further in falsifying history by claiming that he personally brought about Korea's liberation from Japan in 1945 and single-handedly achieved victory over the United States in the Korean War. The Chinese intervention in the Korean War is what actually saved the North, but beginning in the 1960s the North Korean account began eliminating even the contributions of their Chinese allies.

Otherwise, the authoritarian playbook was similar: In order to divert attention away from the people's miseries, the North Korean regime, like that of China, turned to the politics of fear, based on the nation's historical victimization by the outside world. Whether it was the United States, "the West," Japan, or internal enemies collaborating with foreigners, externally generated forces constantly destroyed or threatened to destroy the country in recent history, so said the official perspective.

This required, then, a great leader or a heroic party to repel such forces and overturn historical injustices, but only if the people stood together vigilantly to support that leadership. Such was the approach of totalitarian rulers such as Hitler and Stalin, as well as of Mao and Kim. It depended on a militarized regimentation of society under a personality cult, which usually found its logical end in disastrous military or mobilizing adventures and eventually overrode the rationale for empowering these men in the first place.

Chapter 55

LOTTE BETWEEN KOREA AND JAPAN

The arrest in 2016 of the oldest daughter of the Lotte Group's founder for suspected bribery and other misdeeds represented the latest chapter in the ongoing saga of South Korea's fifth-largest conglomerate company, or *chaebol*. Over the years, it seems most of the major chaebol that dominate the South Korean economy—such as Hyundai, Samsung and Hanjin—have passed through very public struggles among the ruling family members, as if they were staging a television drama from the dynastic past.

Indeed Lotte's aging founder, Shin Kyuk-ho, must have felt like Yi Seong-gye, the founder of the Joseon dynasty, who abdicated in the face of murderous infighting over the throne among his children. Lotte's place in modern Korea carries powerful historical overtones in other ways as well, including the complex hold of traditional family practices and Japan's prominent role in South Korea's economic development.

The story begins in Ulsan, the home region of Shin Kyuk-ho, in the closing years of the Japanese colonial period (1910–1945), when the peninsula was caught in the throes of Japan's war against China and the United States. Back then, Ulsan was not the powerhouse center of industry as it is now, so Shin made his way to nearby Busan, the growing gateway to and, in many ways, product of Japan, in order to attend high school. Upon graduation, he moved to Tokyo to attend Waseda University, somehow avoiding conscription into the battlefront as a student soldier.

This was also when Shin's first daughter, Yeong-ja, was born, with a familiar name for that generation of Korean females, given that it could easily be rendered into a common Japanese name as well. Upon Korea's liberation in 1945, Shin stayed in Japan, joining hundreds of thousands of Koreans who, for whatever reason, made that difficult choice.

He began his company in the late 1940s and chose the name "Lotte" in reference to the love interest ("Charlotte") of Werther, the anxious young protagonist in the famed novel by Goethe. This unusual name for a company thus reflected Japan's outsized role in absorbing and transmitting the globalizing currents of Western culture in the early twentieth century throughout

East Asia, including of course in its colony of Korea. As the young company formed into a producer of confectionaries, particularly chewing gum, in postwar Japan, Shin's two sons, Dong-ju and Dong-bin, were born in the mid-1950s to a Japanese woman, a different mother from that of their older sister Yeong-ja. Nearly thirty years later, they would witness the birth of a fourth sibling, from yet another mother. All of Shin Kyuk-ho's children would take leadership positions in the company, although not surprisingly it would be the two elder sons who held the most power.

As for the company's development, the next major step came following the normalization treaty between South Korea and Japan in 1965, which opened the doors to Japanese investment in its developing neighbor and allowed Shin to expand into his homeland. Thereafter Lotte grew steadily in both countries, particularly South Korea, where the company gained a dominant standing in its original industry of food production. "Shin Ramyun," perhaps its most famous product (along with the ubiquitous "Shrimp Crackers"), used the family's name, which conveniently also means "spicy." But Lotte gained prominence in other industries as well, such as hotels, shopping, resorts, sports (the Lotte Giants of Busan, the counterpart to the Chiba Lotte Marines near Tokyo), and, most impressively, construction. The new Lotte World Tower in Seoul's Jamsil area, next to the Lotte World amusement park, is the culmination and symbol of Lotte Engineering and Construction's extraordinary growth, as it now stands as Korea's tallest skyscraper and one of the tallest in the world.

How a company known for its packaged gum developed into a builder of giant buildings is a story intimately tied to the ways South Korea's economy nurtured the explosive expansion of family-controlled companies through state aid, particularly since the 1960s. These conglomerates also grew through connections to Japan, not only via the normalization of relations in 1965 but the historical basis established by Japan's colonial rule, as seen in the life of Shin Kyuk-ho.

Now his sons, themselves in their 60s and facing legal troubles, are battling for control over the company that their father founded, which is interesting for many reasons, including that Dong-bin, the slightly younger brother, has sought to overturn the traditional Korean preference for the oldest son. But this, too, might reflect Japanese influence. One of the major challenges in Japan's colonial rule, in fact, came in harmonizing the two countries' family customs. The Japanese had great difficulty figuring out the intricacies of traditional Korean practices involving inheritance, adoption, concubines, their children, and how these customs could accommodate newer patterns of divorce and economic activity centered on the nuclear family.

Figure 55.1 Lotte World Tower, southeastern Seoul.

The convergence of these strains appears to have played an important role in the development of Lotte Group up to the present day, as the founder's children struggle over their respective inheritances. It is said that Shin Kyuk-ho made sure to divide his time equally between his residences in Busan and Tokyo in order to reinforce the binational basis of his business empire. His life story, and that of his company, thus highlighted the close interaction between the two countries in South Korea's economic development, but the more recent difficulties also seem to issue reminders of this relationship's complex hardships as well.

Chapter 56

COMFORT WOMEN BEHOLDEN TO HISTORY

It became immediately clear that the agreement between the South Korean and Japanese governments on the "comfort women" issue was driven by the number "2015," at least from the Korean side. It did not take a genius to figure this out. The South Korean foreign minister's opening remarks on December 28, 2015, to announce the accord stated that his government sought to find an "early resolution" to this "most crucial history-related issue" between the two countries. Why the hurry? Because this had to take place before the end of 2015.

That year marked the 50th anniversary of the 1965 treaty to restore diplomatic relations between South Korea and its former colonial master, Japan. Moreover, this 1965 agreement was pushed through over fierce protests by the father of President Park Geun-hye, Park Chung-hee, in order to gain access to money and technology. So the younger Park's motivation was not only to make a symbolic splash, but to reinforce and legitimize that controversial step from a half-century earlier. This effort to justify, enhance and exploit her father's deeds guided Park Geun-hye throughout her administration--to a disastrous point, as it turned out.

There were also other factors behind the comfort women agreement, of course, including geopolitical considerations like the shared fear of a rising China, though this was probably overstated. The influence of the United States, though, is another matter, which continues a long-standing historical pattern. Both South Korea's and Japan's post–World War II external relations have been dominated by the American security alliance.

Likewise, the post-WWII era in both Asian countries has mostly been led by rightist, anti-communist governing orders cultivated in the Cold War. In South Korea, such circumstances allowed regimes to justify their dictatorial rule through the pursuit of intensive economic development. Japan, though not as authoritarian, was nevertheless dominated politically by the Liberal Democratic Party (LDP), which emerged in the aftermath of the US occupation of Japan (1945–1952). In pursuit of their own interests, the Americans who helped establish the postwar Japanese order permitted the LDP and Japanese citizens to overcome their recent past by pretending they had little liability for the actions of the wartime military regime. The 2015 agreement's opening clause on the Japanese side even contains a stunning indication of this view: "The issue of comfort women was a matter which, with the involvement of the military authorities of the day, severely injured the honor and dignity of many women."

This wording suggests strongly that the Japanese governments that pursued military expansionism in the first half of the twentieth century were somehow an aberration, even though many of the same people, including the "emperor" and even Prime Minister Abe Shinzo's grandfather, resumed their leadership roles after the war. Hence these figures, in representing the Japanese people as a whole, did not have to take responsibility for wartime aggression, which allowed certain social actors to spread a severe distortion of what had happened. More recently, Abe and other rightwing Japanese nationalists have become further emboldened due to the Chinese government's own provocative actions to fan nationalist hysteria.

The combustible, dangerous mixture of authoritarianism, historical manipulation and nationalism has been demonstrated in Korea as well, especially in the North but also in the South. Successive southern regimes, beginning with Syngman Rhee and continuing long thereafter, inflamed nationalist passions over historical grievances, many of which were embellished for political purposes. So it is not surprising that the comfort women issue, after it began to be openly acknowledged in the late 1980s, would eventually become politicized. But for the most part, it remained mostly a conflict between private Korean citizens and the Japanese government.

The surviving victims were seeking restitution, to be sure, as they had led terribly difficult lives due to their wartime ordeals, but they also sought justice, which would come only from the Japanese government's official recognition of its responsibility, its legal admission of guilt. Likely, though, no Japanese government will do this, because it would open up a Pandora's box of historical claims from those victimized by the Japanese empire. More importantly, the Japanese government would first have to undergo a fundamental transformation in the way it views the past, particularly World War II. Until then, history will remain a recurring cause of friction with its East Asian neighbors.

So again, we are left to wonder about the sudden urgency of the comfort women matter, on the level of state diplomacy, after more than two decades of no progress. The haste, and perhaps carelessness, with which the Park

Figure 56.1 Exhibit on "Comfort Stations," National Memorial Museum of Forced Mobilization under Japanese Occupation, Busan, South Korea.

Geun-hye administration pursued this resolution in order to meet a spurious 2015 deadline was, as predicted by many, matched by the agreement's lack of durability. Indeed, the agreement lasted only as long as the truncated Park government itself. But perhaps that was the point after all.

Chapter 57

A MODEST PROPOSAL FOR DOKDO

I am probably not alone in now tending to roll my eyes whenever I hear about the latest feud over Dokdo, known as Takeshima in Japan. In the spring of 2017, another controversy arose after the Japanese government approved privately published textbooks that refer to South Korea's control over these rocks as an "illegal occupation."

There was nothing new about any of this, but it was enough for the South Korean government to publicly denounce the measure, which likewise changes nothing. South Korea will continue to possess these islets as its territory, the government and other groups in Japan will make their own counterclaims, and the usual emotions will boil on both sides, only to die down until the next round of verbal back-and-forth.

There is, in other words, a performative quality to this dispute, which has been raging since the 1950s. Weary parties on both sides, from civic organizations to public officials, seem to go through the motions in a tiresome ritual, like young adults in South Korea dragging themselves home to participate in ancestral ceremonies during major holidays.

Therefore, I wish to propose a first step in solving this recurring conflict in the spirit of reconciliation and relief: Quit talking about it. First must be the South Korean government, which has recently doubled down on propaganda efforts, from primary schools undertaking special Dokdo education programs to placards and pamphlets placed in train stations, airports, and even diplomatic compounds in foreign countries. This needs to stop. Lawmakers, civic organizations and private citizens can say what they want, but the South Korean government itself should modestly stay above the commotion, knowing that its control over Dokdo will never be endangered. The Japanese government would then follow suit.

This is unlikely to happen, of course, because the respective territorial claims are based not on practical considerations such as the negligible natural resources in Dokdo's surrounding waters, but rather on good old-fashioned tribalism, mixed surprisingly with the workings of democracy itself. Even if cooler heads prevailed in the two central governments, the hotter heads in legislatures, local governments, and civic organizations, as well as rabble-rousers, will always find a plentiful supply of supporters to incite. And in a democracy, these voices must be accounted for, regardless of how irrational they might appear.

In any case, the solution cannot be an authoritarian one, however tempting that seems. South Korean dictators in the past manipulated public sentiment over this dispute to save or strengthen their rule. This is the kind of governing behavior that South Korea has thankfully moved past. But South Koreans are still bound to a firm belief that Dokdo is somehow an absolute matter of patriotic pride, indeed of historical justice. Thus democracy, in this case, works to resist a more rational, realistic solution. Over in Japan, the bureaucrats probably want to avoid this issue as much as possible, but they must contend with agitated residents in Shimane Prefecture, spineless politicians, and loony right-wing groups, the same ones who go around in black trucks to intimidate voters during election campaigns.

Fortunately, neither Japan nor South Korea is currently under the autocratic grip of demagogues, rulers who stoke nationalist passions to wage war. Indeed true democracies have almost never gone to war against each other, which might be the best justification, out of many, for democracy in the first place. So while the messy workings of democracy prevent this problem from being suppressed, they more than compensate by preventing the same problem from escalating into some crazy explosion. Instead, we are left to pursue an imperfect solution with hopes that, over time, more citizens on both sides will come to realize that this is not a straightforward matter.

Both sides have demonstrated, through careful presentation of historical evidence such as maritime logs, bureaucratic records, and maps, that these islands have long been charted and used by the forerunners to today's respective national governments and peoples. Koreans point to the oldest such documentation, dating all the way back to the Silla era from over a millennium ago, but the Japanese contest the accuracy of such sources. The Japanese, meanwhile, can show that the Empire of Japan formally claimed sovereignty over these uninhabited islets in 1905, the same year Japan defeated Russia in the Russo-Japanese War and thereby gained domination over Korea.

This painful shared history, naturally, explains Koreans' emotional attachment to Dokdo as a symbol of historical rectification. Indeed Japan's disastrous imperial ventures in the early modern period lie at the heart of several territorial disputes with China, Russia and others, and it is a problem without any foreseeable resolution. This does not mean, however, that Japan's neighbors should constantly exploit this resentment, however understandable it is.

A way to break free from such a bind is to pursue forgiveness and reconciliation in full consideration of history's complexities. For the Dokdo issue, the best way forward for the South Korean government, it seems, is to practice restraint in public expression. Let the tourists continue to visit, especially from Japan, under tight controls, and make sure to halt Japanese provocations, such as protest boats approaching from Shimane. But first, stop commenting on it. That would be a big step in looking beyond the familiar terrain.

Chapter 58

THE GENERAL SHERMAN
INCIDENT OF 1866

In reflecting on why the United States and North Korea have seemed so often to stand on the brink of military confrontation, we can start by considering the patterns of American–Korean interactions from the past, and here we must go back a century and a half. The relationship began, in fact, very badly, in the late summer of 1866.

That was when an intruding Western merchant ship, buoyed by the annual monsoons, steamed up the Daedong River to Pyongyang despite stern warnings earlier from Korean authorities to retreat. When the rains subsided, the ship became stuck on a sandbar, and following the failure of negotiations to reach a solution, as well as the foreigners' apparent abduction of a Korean official, Koreans set the ship on fire. Crew members fleeing to shore were all killed.

The American captain, who had led a handful of Western officers and a crew of mostly Malay and Chinese sailors, had commandeered a British ship in Shanghai and, in embarking on a hasty mission to force open Korea to trade relations, renamed the ship the "General Sherman." General William Tecumseh Sherman had been a fierce northern commander in the American Civil War, just concluded the year before in 1865, who had mercilessly torn through parts of the south in one of the war's most memorable episodes.

So began the history of United States–Korean relations, through the provocations of a few delusional Americans convinced they could push themselves into a country about which they knew almost nothing and force its government to change fundamental, long-standing behaviors. In hindsight, this was the height of haughty stupidity, but the lessons apparently were not learned, as a fleet of American marines tried to invade Korea five years later, in 1871, partly to exact vengeance and partly to attempt the same kind of gunboat diplomacy again.

The General Sherman incident helped shape the dominant reaction, among Korea's political and social leaders, to prospects of contact with the outside world. Indeed, earlier that same year the Prince Regent, or Daewongun, who controlled the throne in place of his adolescent son, had ordered a brutal per-secution of Catholics, killing hundreds of believers, including French priests working underground. A French armada hence launched a punitive exped-ition on the west coast, which served only to harden Koreans' resistance.

This tradition, which one might call a xenophobic, isolationist strategy of national preservation, remained strong in Korea, taking various forms. It continued to push for the expulsion of foreign influences, people and ideas at the turn of the twentieth century, even when those interactions were benign or helpful. One might suggest that Koreans' sad history in the early twen-tieth century, when they lost national sovereignty, validated such fears, but one could also argue that those fears prevented Korean leaders from avoiding such terrible outcomes.

The subsequent period of Japanese colonial rule, from 1910 to 1945, further complicated this issue of how to respond to both the dangers and benefits of the outside world, but in any case, the struggle for independence strengthened the appeal of nationalist isolationism. Following liberation, this view thrived in both Koreas, but eventually it became more dominant in North Korea, where it was expressed as the official ideology of "Juche," which can be translated as "self-reliance" or "independence" but has effectively functioned as the legitim-ization of a single family's totalitarian rule.

Among the many historical fabrications pushed by this regime has been the claim that the peasant leader of those Koreans who attacked the General Sherman in 1866 was a direct ancestor of the current North Korean leader. It is a shame that, since historical developments in both countries thereafter have made tensions between the United States and North Korea a recurring reality, such a ridiculous story might as well have been true.

Chapter 59

DEPICTIONS OF THE UNITED STATES

South Koreans' views of the United States have often reflected their perspectives on the history behind this relationship. Of course, there is no uniform "America," despite how public opinion surveys might frame the questions. The perception of America depends on whether one is talking about its military, economic or cultural impact, its people, or the US government and political leadership. And just as there is no single America, "South Koreans" hold a range of viewpoints depending on their age, regional background, level of education, and personal experiences with America or Americans, either in South Korea or abroad. Still, it is remarkable how historical understanding has affected the relative significance of these factors in forming South Koreans' impressions of the United States.

In the opening years of the twenty-first century, anti-American sentiment in South Korea was much stronger than it is today. It is difficult to determine whether such developments affected major political changes or, alternatively, resulted from political actions, but not coincidentally this prevailing skepticism of America corresponded to the presidency of Roh Moo-hyun, elected in 2002. He had campaigned on promises of reassessing the country's ties to the United States and won the election in December amid large demonstrations over two schoolgirls killed accidentally by an American military vehicle. Anti-American passions had been inflamed earlier that year when judges in the 2002 Winter Olympics, hosted by the United States, stripped a Korean speed skater of his gold medal in favor of an American athlete. And such nationalist passions reached a fever peak during the 2002 Korea–Japan World Cup a few months later.

One can argue, however, that anti-Americanism had been building for some time, ever since the 1980s when students and others fighting for democratization believed, in defiance of received wisdom about America, that the United States was complicit in the 1980 Gwangju massacre. This had spurred them to reexamine the comprehensive structural forces behind South Korean society and history, particularly in relation to the United States. They reconsidered, for example, America's role in instigating national division after liberation from Japanese rule in 1945, which led to the 1950–1953 Korean War, and in cultivating South Korean dictatorships thereafter, all the while implanting a systematic dependence on America's Cold War interests.

When these activists later ascended to political and social power during the administrations of Kim Dae Jung and Roh Moo-hyun (1998–2008), they stood at the forefront of questioning the benefits of American influence. One indication came from popular culture, including feature films of the 1990s and 2000s such as "Welcome to Dongmakgol" or "The Host" (*Goemul*), which featured caricatures of evil Americans. More subtle treatments such as "Spring in My Hometown" (*Areumdaun Sijeol*), which was set in the latter stages of the Korean War, explored the extensive scope of South Korean dependence on American power.

Eventually, however, public sentiment appeared to shift again, as demonstrated in the conservative, pro-American presidencies of Lee Myung-bak and Park Geun-hye (2008–2016). Again, we cannot determine the precise causal connection between political transitions and the larger public mood regarding this matter. But it cannot be a coincidence that one of the most popular films of recent times, indeed in South Korean box office history, was "Ode to My Father" (*Gukje Sijang*), released in 2014, the second year of President Park Geun-hye's administration. From beginning to end, "Ode to My Father," though not without some ambiguity, seems to celebrate America's role in South Korean history. Whether so intended, such a version of the past reflects the sentiments of those South Koreans, particularly the older generations, who believe that America saved South Korea in the Korean War and has been the country's great protector and benefactor ever since.

One wonders to what extent this perspective has spread to younger generations as well, but any prevailing South Korean view of America is bound to change, just as it has done several times in the recent past.

Chapter 60

OVERCOMING OLD VIEWS OF KOREA–UNITED STATES TIES

Among the early surprises from newly elected South Korean President Moon Jae-in was his repeating age-old mantras about South Korea's historical bonds with the United States. His previous statements had suggested that, like probably the majority of South Korean adults now, he understood the complexity of America's role in Korean history. But on his trip in June 2017 to Washington DC, tellingly the first foreign capital he visited after taking office, he delivered the cliche of the "blood alliance" that the two countries had forged in the Korean War and maintained thereafter through common interests and ideals.

Disgraced ousted president Park Geun-hye would not have put it differently, nor indeed would have her father, former dictator Park Chung-Hee. For a progressive who had emphasized South Korea's autonomy from the United States, Moon Jae-in sounded remarkably similar to his predecessors. He even appeared to have gotten carried away with nostalgia, triggered by powerful impressions about the United States implanted into most South Koreans of his generation. He also had a familial connection to this mythology, which he was eager to highlight to his American hosts.

As we know, Moon was born near Busan in early 1953, just a couple of years after his parents joined thousands of other civilians fleeing the Chinese advance into the coastal city of Heungnam in late December of 1950, during the early months of the Korean War. They were among over 10,000 refugees allowed to board an American transport ship in what came to be known as the Hungnam Evacuation, or the "Christmas miracle," which provided safe passage to Busan, the temporary capital of South Korea at the time. (The hit film "Ode to My Father" opens with a stirring dramatization of this event.)

This was one of several moments in America's intervention in the Korean War, such as the Incheon Landing of September 1950, that shaped the popular faith in America's salvational role, a picture further promoted by both South Koreans and Americans during the Cold War. With the liberalization that accompanied democratization in the late twentieth century, however,

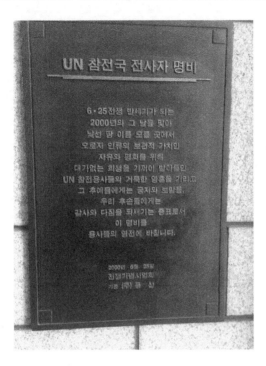

Figure 60.1 Memorial plaque in dedication to the UN forces who participated in the Korean War, War Memorial Museum, Seoul.

Koreans came to learn that this neat image of the United States was dubiously simplistic.

A more complicated, honest and realistic understanding of America's involvement in Korea acknowledges that it did not begin with the Korean War, contrary to what almost all Americans also believe, but rather in the mid-nineteenth century. From then to the period immediately following liberation from Japanese rule in 1945, when the anti-communist US military occupation of southern Korea set the stage for horrific brutalities just before the Korean War, much of this earlier history was not pleasant. Furthermore, the US forces depicted as heroes for rescuing desperate North Koreans in late 1950 subsequently went on to carpet-bomb North Korea indiscriminately, likely killing hundreds of thousands of civilians.

In a terrible irony, these bitter memories allowed the Kim dynasty to fabricate stories about itself in order to cement its grip on the North Korean population. In a tragic way, then, the US military involvement on the Korean peninsula contributed significantly to solidifying the same North Korean regime that everyone now condemns, a regime that can easily point to past American actions as justification for developing its nuclear program.

The other irony is that this more reasonable historical understanding directly arose from the same forces of the democratic opening that produced a
more forthright view of South Korean state violence from the Korean War
era. These atrocities began with the killing of tens of thousands of civilians
on Jeju Island in 1948 and 1949 and culminated in the countless thousands
of innocents executed by President Syngman Rhee's regime, cultivated and
trained by the United States, right after the start of the Korean War. The
numerous family members of the victims, as well as a few survivors, of these
massacres had to wait decades, under South Korean dictatorships backed by
the United States, to gain redress for their suffering.

So it is understandable if many, if not most, South Koreans do not buy into
the ready-made images of American benevolence and of the alliance with the
US. Of course, there is much to be said for the positive aspects of America's
historical impact, which might be considered more important in the end. But
hopefully, regardless of where one falls in the spectrum of opinions about this
topic, everyone can recognize that it was not as simple as what these cere-
monial meetings between political leaders suggest.

Chapter 61

FOREIGN LANGUAGE DEPENDENCY

In a pregame exhibition for the Korean professional baseball All-Star Game in July 2016, a huge target was laid down on the field with very large promotional writing that read, "Tire Bank KBO All-Star Game" and "Bunt King," and nothing else. That is, there was no lettering in the Korean language; in fact, an uninformed viewer would have little reason to know in what country this event was being held.

Many observers over the years have complained about South Koreans' preoccupation with English, but often to bemoan their inability to master the language or to dedicate themselves to it. Perhaps this is the reason for the overcompensation that one finds almost everywhere in South Korean public life, such as television commercials that include English in some form and end with an affected native English voice-over of the product or slogan, as if to provide supreme authenticity. Just as comical are awkward constructions ("Konglish" is the term for these creations) in menu items or signs, as well as strained efforts to use the most exotic or esoteric English words and terms. A case in point: the South Korean baseball team "SK Wyverns," in reference to a creature that, unbeknownst to most English speakers, is something like a dragon.

What appears as slavish devotion to a foreign language, though, is nothing new in Korea. We need only to be reminded of the 1,500 years of Chinese writing's dominance on the peninsula since ancient times, even though the Korean language is about as different from Chinese as it is from English. Granted, there were attempts to adapt Chinese writing to spoken Korean, one of which was Idu, a convoluted system in which individual Chinese ideographs stood for certain Korean syllables. Idu remained in use, at least in bureaucratic documents, up to the early twentieth century, but of course it was not suitable for nonspecialists.

And here we come to perhaps the most important reason behind the long domination of literary Chinese in Korean history: its utility as a marker for prestige and social status. Even after the fifteenth-century invention of the now-celebrated Korean alphabet, which perfectly expressed the Korean language, the alphabet remained mostly unused and unloved by the government and ruling elite. Thankfully the alphabet's extraordinary functionality was exploited and developed by women and other non-elites over the course of the Joseon era, before foreign missionaries, ironically, and Korean reformers at the turn of the twentieth century helped to establish the alphabet's centrality in public life.

But this came four centuries too late. Imagine the scale of social and cultural advancement that could have arisen had Korean leaders embraced the alphabet upon its promulgation in the 1400s. They seemed more interested, however, in strengthening the connection between cultural elitism, represented by literary Chinese, and social and political exclusivity, regardless of how absurdly this bound them, and the country as a whole, to a burdensome writing system. By the time most educated Koreans came around to this reality in the early twentieth century, the Japanese were taking over the country, and thereafter Japanese took the place of Chinese in becoming the written standard for political and cultural authority.

Unlike in the premodern era, however, this development was more clearly a product of foreign coercion, so not surprisingly, after liberation in 1945 Koreans abolished the public appearance of Japanese and promoted use of the Korean alphabet, though to different degrees in the South and North. In South Korea, the ensuing era of American political and cultural influence, a product of military and economic dependence on the United States, brought with it the increasing use of English in public life and the education system as a replacement for Japanese. Naturally, English became even more associated with social prestige and, as was the case in many other countries, the *de facto* universal language through which to connect with the wider world.

Japanese influence, however, remained strong among South Korean elites beneath the surface and behind the scenes. Popular cultural forms, such as television broadcasting, routinely and almost mechanically copied Japanese models, even as Japanese cultural products remained restricted in South Korea until the dawn of the twenty-first century. A prime example of this came from the Korean Baseball Organization (KBO), whose naming practices followed an odd mixture of two foreign conventions, thus reinforcing an embarrassing double dependence. Since its founding in the early 1980s, the league's teams have directly applied the Japanese model, which had resulted from Japan's own dependence on the United States, by using the ownership company's name combined with a nickname in English, such as the "LG Twins" (of Seoul) or the "Samsung Lions" (Daegu). This paved the way toward something like the "SK Wyverns."

Are Korean names and words so devalued that South Korean baseball teams must employ the Japanese example of using English nicknames? I am certainly not in favor of going all nationalistic with this kind of thing, and the use of English in public life serves an important function. But I hope that South Koreans can thoughtfully reconsider their various obsessions with English, which I believe are tied to unhelpful attitudes concerning social status and prestige. Perhaps they can start with baseball, which is very much a native sport now, indeed much more popular in South Korea than in the United States.

Part IX

TRIALS OF MODERNIZATION

Chapter 62

SUMMER SYMMETRIES

It has now been well over a century since Korea was last ruled by a single, native political system, and well over seven decades since liberation from Japanese colonial rule, which was declared on August 15, 1945. But did Korea truly gain liberation? This has been a nagging question since nearly the beginning, for it quickly became clear, after the initial euphoria, that one foreign ruler would be replaced by another.

The partition of the peninsula by the occupying Allied armies in the summer of 1945 would eventually lead to the eruption of the Korean War five summers later in June 1950. After millions of deaths, the armistice of July 1953 halted the fighting and solidified the national division that we still have today. This painful summer symmetry has always dampened a bit the annual observance of Liberation Day, or the "restoration of light" holiday (*Gwangbokjeol*). The connections between these events, after all, are inescapable. But in what way?

If Koreans had known back in 1945 that liberation would result in permanent national division, would they still have welcomed it? This is not a fair or realistic question, of course, but I would think that yes, most would have preferred such an outcome over the continuation of Japanese rule. Furthermore, while citizens of North Korea today might not share this view (one can never know), many if not most South Koreans see little room for uncertainty here. For them, the Korean War and national division were tragedies, to be sure, but over the long term, the "restoration of light" nourished the growth of a modern, free society, at least in the south.

To those who subscribe to this "brighter" view of liberation, August 15 should invite a double celebration, not only of freedom from Japanese rule in 1945, but also of the founding (*geonguk*) of the Republic of Korea, or South Korea, on the same date in 1948. In a ceremony filled with irony, on that day the government of South Korea was formally established in front of the huge building that had served as the headquarters of the Japanese colonial regime and the subsequent American military government. Symbolically, then, South Korea was being launched as the successor to those earlier states more than as a clean break from them.

To top it all off, the new republic claimed sovereignty over the entire peninsula, despite the disturbing realities, which were reinforced just a few weeks later when the North Korean state was itself formally proclaimed. Little wonder, then, that recognition of August 15 as South Korea's "foundation day" has always been relatively muted. And although the founding constitution was formally implemented that summer as well, South Koreans cannot commemorate it because the country's constitution was replaced numerous times thereafter, even by constitutions that legitimated dictatorships. The 1948 document was not one of them, but in Rhee's hands, the government became authoritarian anyway.

This only scratches the surface of the historical complexity of South Korea's beginnings, which perhaps could have implanted a sound democratic order, but instead set the foundation for autocracy and corruption, even before the emergencies of the Korean War. Much of South Korean history thereafter, then, can be considered an extended effort to overturn the shortcomings of the country's birth on August 15, 1948, which in turn was the product of a flawed gestation following the liberation of August 15, 1945. To continue with this uncomfortable analogy, the country's childhood was one of searing trials and tribulation before it finally entered an adulthood marked by a prosperous liberal democracy.

To some, the greatest difficulties of this adolescence came from poverty and looming threats, as represented by the neighbor to the north, and that the strength of South Korea developed from meeting these challenges. To others, the country's maturation came from overcoming, through persistent struggle, the injustices of a system run by a privileged few, and on openly acknowledging the failures and continuing legacy of the past.

To those who hold the latter view, I would ask that this spirit of openness regarding history be extended toward a reconsideration also of the "restoration of light" that occurred through liberation. It has become commonplace, for example, to refer to the colonial experience as a "dark period" (*amheukgi*), as if to accentuate the glow of August 15, 1945. Most academic historians, however, would not consider the entire colonial period a uniformly bleak one, characterized by relentless oppression and sadness. Rather, while not justifying or legitimating Japanese rule, which would be absurd, they recognize that this very important era was marked by major changes and a wide variety of experiences.

In other words, the summers of 1945, 1948, 1950 and 1953 did not spring suddenly and directly from the summer of 1910, the moment of Korea's fall into status as a Japanese colony. A lot happened in those thirty-five years, not all of which can be uniformly categorized as "dark." The challenge for us is to think about what really became illuminated on August 15, 1945, and what threw the nation into the deepening shadows.

Chapter 63

THE KOREAN WAR AS
A TURNING POINT

The annual commemoration of the start of the Korean War on June 25, 1950, always issues reminders of the unfinished business of that war, which officially did not end in 1953; the armistice that stopped the fighting that year did not ensure a permanent peace.

In terms of lives lost and the scale of dislocation, the Korean War might have been the third most destructive war anywhere in the twentieth century. And while at heart a civil conflict, it was also a global event, involving more than twenty-five countries and implanting the Cold War as the dominant international order for decades. After the deaths of millions of soldiers and civilians, the Korean War thus cemented the hostile partition of the penin-sula, a division that would determine the fundamental character of North and South Korea, which for several decades thereafter developed as mirror images of each other in important ways.

In both places, there emerged military dictatorships that legitimized their rule based on mutual hostility. Both regimes also pushed regimented indus-trialization and social control as a counter to the other. South Korea would eventually break free of this pattern, while North Korea would remain in it, with tragic consequences for the North Korean people. Eventually, then, a great historical divergence characterized the long-term outcomes of the two main combatants of the Korean War.

We would benefit, however, from viewing the Korean War as not only the originator of significant developments, but also a culmination of them. In this way, like all great historical events, the Korean War acts as a historical fulcrum or watershed, serving as the result, as well as the origin, of major historical change. Most immediately, the few years preceding the Korean War's outbreak set the stage for its horrors. Upon Korea's liberation from Japanese colonial rule in 1945, the peninsula was divided into the Soviet (north) and American (south) occupation zones. These two conquering superpowers, which did not tolerate opposing ideologies or parties in their respective realms, would set the boundaries and character of politics on the peninsula.

In both territories, though, the native Koreans went far beyond the occupying powers in suppressing and eliminating the opposition. In the North, the landlords, intellectuals, Christians and others objecting to communist rule were killed, harassed or driven south. In the South, the laborers, leftists, and resisting villagers received similar treatment. And despite the efforts of some leaders, politics came to be dominated by uncompromising extremists on both sides. This was the context out of which separate southern and northern states were established in the summer of 1948.

The move to create autonomous Korean states did not bring about a reprieve from the internal conflicts, however, and on both sides, some of the most terrible events took place in the two years leading up to June 1950. The Korean War, then, was in many ways the intensified continuation of the five-year period after liberation. Nevertheless, the brutality increased significantly during the war and spread to countless acts of vicious revenge at the level of neighborhoods and villages. Perhaps this was because the roots of the familial, social, political, and religious cleavages that spawned such atrocities extended further back in time.

Socioeconomic divisions increased throughout the latter part of the preceding Japanese colonial period, particularly in the southern regions, as many villagers fell into impoverished lives as tenants, while some Koreans became very wealthy landlords. The intensive mobilization for Japan's imperialist wars beginning in the late 1930s also brought forth unease and deprivation, further increasing social tension. These circumstances further divided Koreans, in both the urban and rural areas, between those, like the police, who worked for or supported the colonial regime, and those who did not.

Of course one could suggest that the Japanese conquest of Korea would not have happened at all without deep divisions among Koreans at the turn of the twentieth century, and so on. There is no need to continue this mental exercise, however, to remember that the Korean War's historical significance extended far backward as well as forward.

Chapter 64

THE STUDENTS OF APRIL

"April is the cruelest month," wrote T.S. Eliot to begin his epic poem, "The Wasteland." He referred to the often agonizing mixture of "memory and desire" that accompanies the onset of spring, when hopes for a nourishing new beginning—"April showers bring May flowers"—are tempered by experiences of pain and disappointment.

For observers of modern Korean history, these perceptions of both the promise and peril of April often bring to mind the revolution of April 19, 1960, or "Sa-il-gu," when students led mass protests against the corrupt South Korean government of President Syngman Rhee. The demonstrations led to scores of deaths and injuries among the protesters but eventually toppled the regime.

This momentous event also leads us to contemplate the broader role that students have played in South Korea's past. In doing so, we find compelling connections between that fateful moment in spring 1960 to other major events, particularly in the epic of democratization, a story marked by short-term suffering for the sake of long-term gain. The students who led the April 1960 demonstrations came from what can be called "the Korean War generation": They were born at the end of the Japanese colonial period in the throes of wartime mobilization, the deprivations of which many of them likely remembered.

In fact, some may have even attended school before the liberation in 1945, although school had been out of reach for most Koreans at the time. Their childhoods were marked by the dislocations of the subsequent postliberation period, which led directly to the Korean War. Their adolescence came amid the devastation and calamities of the Korean War, and then was seared by the challenges of reconstruction in the 1950s.

Not all was bleak, however, for the 1950s also molded the students into the first generation to become educated *en masse* through public schooling and, just as importantly, through the widespread use of the Korean alphabet. The world of knowledge opened up to them, and they gained an awareness of the connections between their experiences and the larger issues of the day.

Figure 64.1 Entrance to the April 19th Memorial Hall, downtown Seoul.

This awakening prompted them to march through the streets in 1960, when a clearly rigged national election dashed their hopes for a better, more just Korean society. But their accomplishments that fateful spring would lay the groundwork for fundamental change through student leadership for the remainder of the century. Students, both in college and high school, began protesting in the southern city of Masan in March 1960 following the killing of Gim Ju-yeol, a local high school student, by the police. This eventually sparked demonstrations around the country, especially in the capital city.

It was this same spirit of student activism, led by some of the same student leaders, that spurred the marches the following year calling for an immediate resolution to national division. In response, major general Park Chung-Hee staged a *coup d'etat* in May 1961 that quickly ended the Korean experiment in democracy. The students, however, were not stopped. They joined a powerful movement of student unrest around the world in the 1960s, as they would rise up again to lead mass protests against the normalization of relations with Japan in the mid-1960s and against a constitutional amendment legalizing a third consecutive presidential term for Park in 1969.

After absolutist rule ("Yushin") was implemented in 1972, the students remained at the forefront of resistance, joined by laborers, religious leaders, intellectuals and others. Their work cemented the role of student leadership in the democratization movement throughout the 1970s and 1980s, during which the end of Park's dictatorship led to yet another one through the bloody suppression of student-initiated demonstrations in the city of Gwangju in the spring of 1980. Finally, in the spring of 1987, the students led the break-through to electoral democracy by serving again as the shock troops of mass street protests.

Throughout their terrible ordeals, including unrelenting harassment, arbi-trary arrests, routine beatings and horrific bouts in prison when they were tortured, the students persisted. Although they were not the only ones who made great sacrifices for the greater good, South Koreans could not have achieved democratization without them. The students of April, in other words, nurtured the soil for the May flowers of democracy.

Chapter 65

THE FOUR Ds OF SOUTH KOREAN HISTORY

If one were to write a history of South Korea, he or she would have to start with a big decision: What should be the "master narrative" of this period of over seven decades? In other words, how does one best tell the larger story of South Korea's historical experience?

This choice would reflect the author's evaluation of the most valuable factors and events, but also the sense of a broader purpose of historical change, and a judgment on the country today. The values and ideological stance of the author, in short, would play a large role in determining this master narrative. Still, it seems one can narrow down the choices for this grand theme to the four Ds: Development, Dictatorship, Democratization and Division.

Development refers to the extraordinary pace and scale of economic change, particularly since the 1960s when growth through export-oriented industrialization began as a national strategy. From being one of the poorest countries in the world in the 1950s, amid recovery and reconstruction from the Korean War, within half a century South Korea became one of the most economically advanced. By every measure, the material changes were precipitous and fundamentally altered the lives of South Koreans. This development also encompassed urbanization and population growth, a proliferation of occupations, basic transformations in society and culture, and a political system that was measured according to economic growth.

This is also why the second possible master narrative, *dictatorship*, remains very convincing. Few observers would suggest that dictatorship should be celebrated, of course. But if one believes that only a strongman, like Syngman Rhee or Park Chung-Hee, could have brought the necessary order and direction to a country ravaged by colonialism and civil war, then dictatorship can appear as a necessary ingredient to the pursuit of economic growth. Autocratic rule in South Korea, after all, did not produce the totalitarian brutality seen in so many other countries of the twentieth century, so the reasoning goes. As painful as they might have been, the excesses of authoritarian politics constituted sacrifices, or perhaps necessary evils, for the sake of achieving economic growth and social stability. Even democracy, from this perspective, had to wait until this combination of stability and growth under dictatorship could mature.

For many others, however, *democratization* could have been realized much earlier without sacrificing economic development or social stability. Stability under dictatorship, furthermore, was but an illusion, for throughout the four decades of autocracy South Koreans fiercely resisted the dictators, along with the corruption and injustices that were inherent to their rule. It was neither dictatorship nor even economic development, then, but rather the people's continuing struggle to overcome political and economic inequality that makes up the great story of South Korean history. This view also contains an inclination to find a clear direction in national history, a great collective cause for which the nation strived and finally achieved a breakthrough, though perhaps incompletely or imperfectly, in 1987.

In a way similar to the goal-oriented view that sees economic development as having justified all the history that preceded it, a people-centered perspective tends to view the entirety of modern Korean history through the lens of democratization. The origins of this eminent enterprise, then, are not necessarily located in South Korean history, but rather in the independence struggle against Japanese colonialism in the early twentieth century, or even further back, in the Donghak Uprising of 1894, for example.

Hence, even for those who favor democratization as the master narrative, there is a fourth theme that might ultimately be the most significant: *division*. For all the pride that accompanies the achievement of democracy or industrialization, the greater task of overcoming national division remains. From this view, national division determined most the direction of South Korean history, particularly in the realms of politics and international relations.

This division was induced and reinforced by the domination of the Cold War international order under which South Korea was formed in 1948 and developed thereafter. National division then functioned as legitimation for the dictatorships, which pushed a feverish anti-communism as a way to justify their crackdowns on political dissent. And this fear and loathing of North Korea continue somewhat to drive social and ideological divisions within South Korea today. For all these reasons, one cannot think about, much less write about, the history of South Korea without accounting for the commanding impact of national division.

Interestingly, however, those who argue for the dictatorship or development theme (or, more frequently, both) might agree with such a premise: Fueled by the horrific memories of the Korean War, the threat of North Korea was indeed the predominant reality that framed the history of South Korea, up to the present day. But this combination of dictatorship and development produced, in the end, the greatest achievements of South Korean history. In this view, such a South Korea should be celebrated as a vibrant, wealthy, and yes, democratic society that survived and ultimately thrived under the grave conditions of national division.

Chapter 66

TWO ASSASSINATIONS

Probably the most remarkable coincidence in Korean history involved a pair of momentous assassinations: of Ito Hirobumi on October 26, 1909, and of Park Chung-Hee exactly seventy years later. The compelling connections between the two figures, however, go beyond the parallels in their deaths.

One could make a convincing argument that Ito was the most influential person, for good or bad, in Japan's rise as a major power in the early twentieth century. From a rather modest background as a lower status samurai in western Japan, he played an instrumental role in modernizing his homeland after the overthrow of the shogun's rule in 1868. He visited Western countries on multiple occasions and helped incorporate ideas and models from the outside world into Japan's political system, including its constitution. And in 1885, he became Japan's first prime minister, a title he would hold on several other occasions, and thereafter remained at the center of his country's emergence as Asia's most economically and militarily advanced country.

Ito's association with Korea resulted from Japan's growth into an imperialist power with designs on neighboring territories, especially Korea. It was for the purpose of dominating Korea that Japan successfully waged wars, in and around the peninsula, against China and Russia at the turn of the twentieth century. It was also for this purpose that, following Japan's defeat of Russia in 1905, Korea was forced into status as a protectorate, with the Japanese taking control of the Korean government's financial and foreign affairs. This was how Ito came to Korea, as the first commander, or Resident-General, of the Japanese protectorate government. Through this position Ito pushed through many changes and led the gradual strengthening of Japan's grip over the peninsula, even forcing a change in the Korean monarchy in 1907.

Though he was assassinated a few months after he left this post in 1909, many Koreans still regarded him as the prime instigator of the Japanese takeover. His assassin, An Jung-geun, gunned him down at a train platform in Manchuria, and this likely accelerated Japan's annexation of Korea, which occurred in the summer of 1910. That such a central figure in modern Japanese history ended up dying at the hands of a Korean assassin was a shameful irony, of course, since it was Ito who had led the development of Japan into an imperialist power in the first place. From the Korean perspective, it was not Ito the man as much as Ito the symbol that counted. Hence, An Jung-geun has been hailed as a great national hero, an emblem of Koreans' patriotic passions, righteous resistance and fighting spirit.

This stands in stark contrast to the popular perspective on Gim Jae-gyu, the man who pulled the trigger on President Park Chung-Hee on the same date seventy years later. If Ito's killing was a great irony, Park's assassination in 1979 was even more so. It took place amid widespread anti-government protests in the southeastern cities of Busan and Masan in the fall of 1979. These demonstrations were the culmination, in many ways, of a rising tide of resistance against the "Yushin" dictatorship that Park had implemented in 1972. As people wondered how Park would respond to the demonstrations and who would be punished, it turned out that Park himself would be the most prominent victim, not only of the protests, but of the dictatorship as a whole. This is because Gim Jae-gyu, his assassin, was the head of the Korean Central Intelligence Agency, or KCIA, which like other secret police agencies kidnapped and tortured dissidents and resistors. His shooting of Park would be akin, then, to Ito's being shot by one of his long-time Japanese advisors.

Like An Jung-geun, Gim was soon executed for his crime. In his interrogation and trial, Gim insisted that he wanted to prevent social chaos and promote democracy. But as a chief enforcer of the authoritarian regime, his words and motives justifiably were viewed with great suspicion. The manner in which he carried out his offense bothered people as well: He did so at a small, private gathering, and his intent originally was to kill not Park but rather his chief bodyguard, whom Gim personally despised. Finally, Gim's actions did not bring about social stability or democracy (at least not immediately), but rather another military dictatorship and a great deal of bloodshed the following year.

That An Jung-geun, unlike Gim Jae-gyu, is held in such high esteem is understandable, given the complicated, painful and often terrible role played by Japan in Korea's modern history. Still, it is a little disturbing that a man best known as an assassin enjoys such a lofty standing. The South Korean postal service has even issued commemorative postage stamps in An's honor, on multiple occasions. A further twist is that the date itself, "10–26," is better known for Gim's deed than An's. This is likely because the center of attention for the earlier event is the perpetrator, whereas for the latter event, it is the victim. Political assassinations are not unique to Korea, but the curious way by which they are viewed is indeed very much a product of Korea's particular historical circumstances.

Chapter 67

ROADS TO REVOLUTION

In 2016, the word "revolution" began to circulate in reference to massive street demonstrations ("candlelight revolution"), as well as to the unprecedented reach of investigative journalism concerning President Park Geun-hye and her circle. Indeed the label of "revolution" has been applied to many moments in the country's history, but one could argue that South Korea actually has never undergone a genuine revolution.

A revolution brings about an abrupt overturning of the social order, an upending of the manner by which privilege (political, economic, or otherwise) is exercised, and the overthrow of the ruling group(s) that long enjoyed such advantages. In this sense, the modern world has witnessed many definitive revolutions, including the French Revolution of 1789, anti-colonial revolutions that established nation-states in the Americas, and the communist revolutions of the twentieth century beginning with Russia in 1917. The latter group also includes North Korea's revolution in the 1940s and 1950s and two revolutions in China: the communist victory over the nationalists in 1949 and the Cultural Revolution of the 1960s and 1970s.

As the Chinese and North Korean examples suggest, such revolutions have had a mostly dismal record. Often, the popular rage that fueled the revolution led to excesses on the other side, including mass murder, starvation, or totalitarianism. This is also why wars and brutal violence have usually accompanied revolutions. In this regard, claims of "revolution" in Korea put forth by historical actors or history books seem exaggerated, including references to the March First Independence Movement against Japanese rule in 1919, the April Student Revolution of 1960, or the "military revolution" of 1961. And neither the democratization of 1987 nor the industrial and digital revolutions in the economy appear to have produced a firmly equitable social order.

These transitions, however, did contribute to the gradual progression in modern Korea toward greater social equality and mobility, a process that was nevertheless marked by setbacks as well as advances. Urgent domestic reforms in response to rebellions in the late nineteenth century, a reflection of accumulating social injustices, proved insufficient to save the Joseon dynasty from the forces of imperialism. The ensuing period of Japanese occupation, beginning in 1910, accelerated some of the earlier liberalizing trends but also instituted a military dictatorship that cultivated social privileges dependent on colonial rule.

Following the 1945 liberation, which significantly did not result from the Koreans' own efforts—however laudable they may have been—in South Korea, at least, the elites who arose under foreign occupation mostly stayed in their privileged positions. The circumstances of the Cold War made this possible, but the Korean War, another byproduct of the Cold War, also loosened the firm grip of landed wealth in the countryside, an enormous change. Thereafter, urbanization and universal access to education further hastened social renovation, enough to help drive the overthrow of Syngman Rhee's dictatorship in 1960. This student-led effort was branded a "revolution" at the time, and it very well could have generated revolutionary developments, particularly in democratization.

But we will never know, because the new democratic system was quickly ousted by a military coup in 1961. As with strongmen who took power around the modern world, this coup's leaders branded their deed "revolutionary." But it changed neither the basically autocratic nature of the political system nor the means, reliant heavily on favoritism and corruption, by which certain groups of people gained and protected their privileged standing. Indeed, family-run conglomerates (*chaebol*) that grew enormously through state patronage came to dominate the economy and extended the cultures of exploitation and polarization. On the other hand, urbanization, growth in compulsory education, and increasing exposure to the outside world continued apace, and in combination with the material outcomes of industrialization, they inspired a popular determination to achieve democracy.

The democratization of 1987, the near-revolutionary result of unprecedented street protests, could have been the signal moment of South Korean history. It represented a more substantial, second attempt at democracy, after the brief chance in 1960–1961, but perhaps it could not have been the final one. This is because, as subsequent developments made clear, political democratization did not necessarily produce economic democratization. Even the financial crisis of 1997, which resulted in the breakup of some big conglomerates and the restructuring of others, failed to fundamentally weaken the hold of big business or even its close integration with the state.

These structural factors, along with deeply ingrained mentalities and habits that attend them, are difficult to overcome. Such is the somber reality now facing societies that overthrew communist dictatorships in the 1990s and Arab dictatorships more recently. And this is why the latest "revolutionary" efforts in South Korea in 2016 strived toward a third attempt, or the third stage, of democratization—one that establishes a more comprehensively fair and open society by rooting out, for good, the stubborn, shadowy remnants of unjust privilege. Success along these lines would allow South Koreans to finally realize a true revolution, one gained not as quickly as ideally desired, but one that still can endure over the long term.

Chapter 68

DRAMATIZATIONS OF THE GWANGJU UPRISING

The Gwangju Uprising May 1980 remains one of the signal moments in South Korean history. Although it ended in a massacre of hundreds, the uprising also sparked a concerted civic movement that eventually overthrew the military dictatorship and instituted democratization in 1987.

A measure of Gwangju's epic scope and standing is the enormous number of academic studies, seminars, testimonies, documentaries, novels and dramatizations in popular culture dedicated to commemorating its historical impact. In reflecting on this event and on the "memory industry" that has developed around it, the following reviews some of the most stimulating cinematic treatments:

Hour Glass (*Morae Sigye*, 1995). Featuring the first mainstream visualization of the Gwangju Uprising, this television miniseries set records in viewership, coming as it did less than a decade following the political liberalization of 1987. The main characters converge in Gwangju early in the story. Their respective experiences—with one friend sent into the city as a paratrooper and another becoming an eyewitness from the vantage point of the citizenry—would in many ways determine their futures for the rest of the 1980s.

"Hour Glass" explicitly showed the chaotic brutality of the uprising, with ordinary citizens being subjected to ruthless beatings and killings, which nevertheless served not to subdue them but rather to embolden them in defense of their human dignity. This drama also joined, in the mid-1990s, a broader reckoning of the country's authoritarian past, including the public trial (and conviction) of former presidents Chun Doo-hwan and Roh Tae-woo, the duo in command of the military at the time of the Gwangju Uprising.

A Petal (*Kkonnip*, 1996). Based on Choe Yun's extraordinary short story, "A Petal," like "Hour Glass," depicts the violence viscerally, in fact even more so, through the story of a teenage girl who wanders around like a zombie following her traumatic experience of Gwangju, when she lost her mother and her sanity. And like "Hour Glass," the lingering effects of Gwangju mark the depth of destruction visited not just upon the immediate victims but upon larger society.

Peppermint Candy (*Bakha Satang*, 1999). As with the first two works, "Peppermint Candy" anchors a person's life in the formative experience of Gwangju. But the violence of the event, so prominently displayed in other dramatizations, is mostly just alluded to in "Peppermint Candy." As a fresh-faced new recruit in the army, the main character is sent down to the city in May 1980 to join the military suppression of the demonstrations. There he accidentally shoots a school girl, and the film shows how that one moment triggered a process that would turn an innocent young man into a personifi-cation of the military dictatorship, which he joins as a policeman soon after Gwangju.

Over the course of the next twenty years, he becomes increasingly callous, brutal and unpleasant until he eventually loses everything. His moral degrad-ation is shown through the film's reverse narrative, with each succeeding epi-sode, connected symbolically and visually by trains, going further back in time, all the way to that fateful moment in Gwangju. The result is an extraordinary rendering of the traumatic power of history.

The Old Garden (*Oraedoen Jeongwon*, 2007). As in "Peppermint Candy," the Gwangju scene from 1980 is relatively brief, and the damage from the event unfolds over the long term in the two main characters, whose romantic rela-tionship is sacrificed for the sake of continuing the struggle against dictator-ship. Based on a novel by Hwang Seog-yeong, "The Old Garden" constantly shifts between the contemporary time of late 1990s South Korea and the early- to mid-1980s.

This gap corresponds roughly to the seventeen years the main character spends in jail for his leadership role in the resistance. Over that period, the woman from whom he is separated also suffers, both from having to raise their daughter alone and from taking his place in the democracy movement, an experience that leaves her increasingly disillusioned and skeptical about its worth. Unlike most of the other cinematic portrayals of Gwangju's his-torical significance, then, "The Old Garden" actually is ambivalent about the ultimate value of the anti-dictatorship struggle, especially when the costs of the personal sacrifice extend beyond one's self. It is, in sum, a somber reflection on the larger meaning of South Korea's democratization and modernization.

May 18 (*Hwaryeohan Hyuga*, 2008). The most thorough cinematic recreation of the Gwangju Uprising appears in "May 18," which follows a family and its circle of friends through the entire event, from its beginnings as a student dem-onstration to its fiery end ten days later. Central to the depiction of this process is the theme of personal loss, highlighted through two narrative motifs: that of

Figure 68.1 May 18 National Cemetery, Gwangju, South Korea.

separated brothers, which for understandable reasons is a recurring element in dramatizations of the Korean War; and of romantic love cut short by larger circumstances, a staple of Korean melodrama.

In this way, "May 18" is mostly a conventional dramatization, but one that offers a panoramic view of all the main forces—political, military, social, cultural—that converged in that space at that time, forces that also dominate the memory of South Korean history as a whole.

A Taxi Driver (*Taeksi Unjeonsa*, 2017). The latest cinematic recreation follows a Seoul cab driver hired by a German reporter to take him to Gwangju soon after the uprising begins. They sneak their way into the besieged city, where they encounter—and document—both the brutalities of the government forces and the humanity of the citizens. Together this pair smuggles out the film footage and photographs showing what really was taking place, which would prove crucial to driving the democratization movement in South Korea thereafter.

Featuring Song Gang-ho in the title role, "A Taxi Driver" presents a riveting story focused on not just the violence and cruelty, but also the everyday normality of those caught up in such an epic moment in history. This demonstrates how the stakes for all South Koreans, not just those in Gwangju, were ultimately tied to what was taking place in one harrowing corner of the country.

Chapter 69

THE GREAT LABOR UPRISING OF 1987

What is often overlooked in commemorating the democratization of 1987 is that the process did not stop with, or was limited to, political liberalization, but included an equally extraordinary mass movement for economic democratization. Stimulated by the events of June, in early July 1987 workers at Hyundai Engines in Ulsan established an independent union in order to demand, collectively, higher wages and better working conditions, as well as the right to organize. This spark led to an epochal firestorm of worker actions across the country that became known historically as the Great Labor Uprising of 1987.

The period between July and September of 1987 witnessed the eruption of over 3,000 strikes and other protests, along with countless new independent unions leading hundreds of thousands of participating workers. In reflecting the reach of the political democratization of June, employees in a wide range of sectors, from bus and cab drivers to journalists and TV producers, established "democratic unions," associations, and other organizations to claim their economic rights and push for fairer treatment. But it was the factory workers who drove this relentless activity, particularly those who worked for large companies such as the ones in Hyundai Group.

While the founders and managers of these conglomerates gained fame and credit for South Korea's economic "miracle," their workers served as the foundation of this development for decades under difficult working conditions, with few rights and almost no chances for independent collective action. The authoritarian governments had firmly clamped down on any such possibilities, instead promoting sham company unions that did the bidding of management and, ultimately, the state. Leaders in these two sectors pursued the common interest of maintaining the system of exploiting Korean workers with low wages.

The workers did not necessarily cower, however. Throughout the dictatorship era, laborers ceaselessly attempted to organize themselves, from protests in individual sweatshops to unions representing entire factories or companies. But they were almost always beaten down, often quite literally, by mass firings, threats, and the mobilization of police and thugs. The workers' battles, in other words, were part of the broader struggle for democracy.

Little wonder, then, that the Great Labor Uprising of 1987 took place immediately on the heels of the political democratization of June; after all, it was freedom of association, in line with the declared new guarantees of speech, assembly, and due process that allowed collective action to truly be effective. Labor leaders now felt emboldened to join together with fellow workers in the same conglomerate or region, or in the same industries nation-wide, to create even bigger organizations and thereby further strengthen their collective power.

By mid-July, workers in other Hyundai factories began their own demo-cratic unions and went on strike to gain concessions from management for wage increases, job security, humane working conditions, and recognition of their rights to organize. Although the Hyundai unions, the ones who sparked this phenomenon, grabbed the headlines by being concentrated in a specific region in the southeast, they inspired and assisted organizing and labor actions all across the country. Employees of the Daewoo shipyard and automobile plant, for example, organized their own democratic unions, as did other employees throughout the economy. By September, over three million workers had participated in strikes, work stoppages, demonstrations and other actions, which doubled the number over the previous ten years combined.

The enormous scale, ferocity and apparent suddenness of these actions brought about a generally negative, disapproving tone in the country's media coverage. And political leaders, even those who had been at the forefront of demanding political freedoms, warned of the ominous consequences of these disruptions for the economy. But without this wave of worker activism in the face of constant physical and other suppression, the laborers who had so long sacrificed for their employers would not have made the breakthrough toward gaining fair treatment and recognition of their economic rights. In other words, without the Great Labor Uprising, the democratization of 1987 would have been incomplete, perhaps even meaningless.

Over the subsequent three-plus decades, the South Korean labor movement has grown and developed in accordance with many factors, and this history can be viewed in differing ways. But undoubtedly, workers, particularly those in the major compounds of Korean industry, enjoy far greater benefits, rights and influence than in 1987, and South Korean unions as a whole are more powerful than their counterparts in many other advanced economies. And despite the alarming increase in wealth polarization in South Korea, the gap between workers and executives in most enterprises remains relatively low, especially compared to places like the United States.

According to the Organization for Economic Co-operation and Development (OECD), the United States, with a traditionally weak labor movement that has gotten only weaker as time has passed, is the most economically unequal society among developed countries. This explains considerably America's ongoing political turmoil. And this is why, in commemorating South Korea's 1987 democratization, we should honor the momentous significance of that summer's Great Labor Uprising as well.

Part X

GRIPPED BY THE PAST

Chapter 70

NATURAL DISASTERS AND THE FALSE WISDOM OF THE PAST

In Korea's dynastic era, natural disasters were treated as warnings and punishment for human behavior, which supported the general belief that people's lives were firmly tied to the heavens. This notion was especially convincing when calamities came in rapid succession, as nearly everyone, from the king and his ministers down to the masses, scrambled to figure out whose moral failings (usually the king and his ministers) or life difficulties (such as commoners' hardships) might have been the cause. Clearly, heaven was expressing displeasure.

This brings to mind the droughts and locust swarms that appear as God's interventions in the Bible, but drawing such a connection between natural phenomena and a greater disturbance in the moral order was fairly standard in the premodern world. And as suggested by the biblical stories, in agricultural societies, the most feared consequence of heavenly punishment was crop failure. During the Joseon era in Korea, from the fourteenth to nineteenth centuries, meticulous government records noted countless instances of earthquakes (over a thousand, almost all minor), severe storms and flooding, and other natural disorders to which were assigned cosmological significance. But it was prolonged drought that raised the most alarm. In response, the Joseon government constructed ditches, levies and reservoirs to better prepare for the next emergency.

But for immediate relief, the king himself, along with officials around the country, undertook very public rituals to pray for rain. The state also released prisoners, rescinded tax and labor burdens, and took other measures to demonstrate remorse. The monarch's legitimacy, after all, was at stake: Given that his authority ultimately emanated from heaven, his personal shortcomings could be the reason for such suffering visited upon his people. As we now know, those natural disasters in the past had nothing to do with human activity. The irony, of course, is that today people indeed are a cause, for human-induced climate change has increased the severity of storms, floods and droughts. But the point is that people back then drew a false connection between the human and natural worlds.

A larger lesson to derive from this point is that the great wisdom of the past often was not very wise. The most influential social actors in the glorified past, such as royalty, the aristocracy, scholars, clerics and philosophers, were usually the same people who believed and taught that eclipses were omens of revolutions and typhoons signaled God's anger. They had no clue about the origins of diseases or species, could not imagine something like plate tectonics, and gained little insight into the reality behind what they directly observed and experienced. They even had no idea where the sun went at night, because to most of them it appeared that the sun revolved around the earth, not the other way around. So in the absence of verifiable knowledge, past wise men invented stories that could perhaps make some sense.

These same political, cultural and social leaders, however, also peddled convenient explanations that justified and solidified their privileges. Those who led governments, wrote books, and led rituals were, for the most part, the same ones who perpetrated social orders that enforced slavery, exploitation and the degradation of women, children and the majority of the people belonging to the underclass.

Korea was not at all distinctive in this regard, of course, and we should be careful not to blindly apply today's moral standards to the distant past. But we also should not get carried away with venerating past "heroes" or ideas that have readily become mythologized for later political purposes, such as nationalism or the legitimization of dictatorships. Every country does this to a certain extent because the manufacturing of historical myths might help fortify a collective sense of identity and civic morality (though this is disputable).

Such exercises of worshipping the past, however, usually sacrifice historical reality, which is that for most of human history people behaved and believed in ways that today we find appalling, justifiably. There might indeed have been some great sages in ancient times, but this should not lead us to romanticize, much less deify, historical figures and primeval wisdom. Such a fixation on the ancients, in fact, is what the ruling orders of previous civilizations promoted, usually for unsavory purposes.

As a historian, the last thing I want to do is to de-emphasize the significance of history, which is endlessly fascinating and worthy of study, but I hope we can keep demythologizing the past as well. We can start by resisting the glorification of ideas from people who enslaved their fellow human beings, endorsed exploitation and mistreatment, and did not know what caused typhoons and earthquakes.

Chapter 71

ROYAL DANGERS

Efforts to demythologize celebrated historical figures and designated national heroes, and therefore also to resist glorifying history, must include the kings and queens, princes and princesses who populate the popular impressions of the past.

As we all know, monarchies were nearly universal in premodern civilizations. There were differences in the degree to which monarchs wielded their authority, just as there was a wide range in their effectiveness and virtuousness. But all monarchies operated on the basic principle of hereditary political power, and this explains why most rulers were anywhere from bad to terrible, some even evil.

Korea was no different. A distinctive feature of Korea's past was the durability of its ruling families, or "dynasties," as both the Goryeo and Joseon kingdoms lasted around five centuries each, providing together a millennium of apparent stability. One can suggest that this outcome was due to inherent advantages in the monarchy system, but there were many contributing factors, including sheer luck. Plus, the Goryeo monarchy was not as steady as it seems, for its authority was usurped by both internal (military officials) and external (Mongols) actors for two centuries combined.

Even for the succeeding Joseon dynasty, which began in the late fourteenth century and ruled the country until the turn of the twentieth century, we are left to wonder how many of the monarchs truly came close to greatness. Most Koreans know about King Sejong ("the Great"), and depending on evaluation criteria we might also name kings such as Seongjong, Yeongjo, or Jeongjo. But this would still constitute a small portion of the twenty-seven Joseon monarchs. Again, the odds of any particular king becoming a wise, just and effective ruler were small—no better, really, than the chances of any other person with privileged upbringing.

The legitimacy of all of these kings, in other words, came not from their virtue or skill but from the accident of birth, their status as biological descendants of a dynastic founder who took power through military force.

Some of them displayed real talent, but this too was a matter of chance, and the system as a whole depended on the mistreatment of most of the people.

Again, this is not to denigrate the bygone era of kingship by sweepingly applying modern notions of social morality, but rather to issue the reminder that these monarchies were more or less hereditary dictatorships. In turn, they relied on a class of elites who also inherited their privileges and maintained them through what we would today recognize as exploitation and abuse. This is why monarchies in some countries today are simply covers for authoritarian rule, or why dictatorships often take the form of monarchies, minus the crowns and flowing robes (think North Korea).

This is also why attempts to maintain some form of monarchy within a parliamentary democracy usually produce thorny issues of sovereignty (Japan, Britain, or countries in the British Commonwealth) or royal families who are mostly powerless, yet still so pampered, that the whole thing becomes somewhat absurd (Spain, Thailand). As astute citizens in those democracies have noted, it's time to finally do away with such an anachronism.

The reason why most of these countries, though, cannot completely escape their long histories of royalty is because a substantial number of regular people seem to be gripped by a powerful nostalgia, or yearning, for precisely what their forebears collectively rejected in the transition to the modern era. They couch such desires for keeping their kings and queens in terms of maintaining core elements of their national history, culture and identity, but I suspect that two very contemporary phenomena also drive this infatuation with monarchy.

First is the power of national historical myths that glamorize past monarchs and their seemingly gilded eras. Such a deception even persists among formerly subjugated peoples. A perfect example is the United States, which despite having been formed in rebellion against the British monarchy in the eighteenth century, still contains large numbers of people who are obsessed with the British royal family, perhaps to an even greater degree than Britons themselves. One only has to sample news stories and the popular media to detect this mass demand for the latest on Prince this and Duchess of that.

In the early twentieth century, following the Joseon kingdom's conquest by the Japanese empire, Korean independence activists, presumably reflecting widespread popular sentiment, rejected the notion of reviving the Korean monarchy. But today's South Koreans seem to possess a fervor for the glamorous presentation of their monarchical past, if judged by trending popular culture.

This may be harmless, but it paves the way for the more dangerous factor behind the persistent lure of monarchies: the longing for a simple solution to complicated problems and social divisions, a solution that promises order in return for a strongman. Full of himself, such a would-be monarch builds a personality cult and spouts chauvinistic distortions of both the past and present. One found this dynamic at work in the 2016 presidential election of the United States, the world's oldest democracy but one still vulnerable to such a danger. As South Koreans continue to develop their own democracy, they would benefit from remaining suspicious of anyone trying to restore monarchy in the guise of stability and national glory.

Chapter 72

NORTH KOREA'S ALTERNATIVE HISTORY

Concern and fascination, mixed with some gallows humor, characterized the popular reaction to the 2017 poisoning of Kim Jong-nam, the older half-brother of North Korean leader Kim Jong-Un. To observers familiar with the bizarre North Korean transplantation of very traditional behavior into a modern authoritarian state, this made some sense. Still, the killing of an exiled potential claimant to the throne, which happened occasionally in Korea's dynastic past, seems to have come straight out of a movie or television drama.

The more fitting genre is probably the dystopian novel, especially George Orwell's "1984," originally published in the 1940s. Orwell's work surged in popularity in the United States more recently in conjunction with the rise of would-be autocrat Donald Trump. No place, however, has replicated the horrific world of totalitarianism, in which every corner of life lies open to surveillance and control by the mechanisms of dictatorship, more than North Korea. And it starts with the Orwellian Big Brother, whose absolute authority justifies and determines every form of cultural, political, social, even familial interaction.

North Korea is now under the reign of its third Big Brother, but he is also the grandson of the original and the son of the successor. This hereditary feature of the strongman system shows that the monarchy has been revived in North Korea, but we should not assume that this country was somehow destined to repeat age-old Korean historical patterns. Indeed the basis of its founding was completely foreign, namely the Allied powers' defeat of Japan in World War II and the postliberation occupation of Korea's northern half by the Soviet Union in 1945. The Soviets did not have to pick Kim Il-Sung as their native leader, but Kim was a reliable communist and had become known to some as an anti-Japanese guerrilla leader from the late 1930s. So this necessary connection to the resistance against colonial rule somewhat limited the Soviets' choices.

Thereafter, Kim Il-Sung chose to solidify his power through ruthless purges, military adventurism (the Korean War), and a hyper-nationalist legitimization narrative based on patently inflated claims about himself. This came straight out of the modern dictator's playbook circulating around the world, but it did not necessarily have to turn out this way.

Over the course of North Korea's early history, from the mid-1940s to the 1960s, many idealistic Koreans who chose to live in the North sincerely believed that it could become the shining alternative to South Korea, which seemed dependent on American-led capitalist imperialism. North Korea would achieve the longed-for independence from external forces as well as liberation from backward Korean traditions, especially the terrible inequities that had long plagued the country. And in contrast to the South, North Korea would be truly democratic, giving voice to the downtrodden and spreading the virtues and fruits of an egalitarian society and economy.

The first signs that such ideals were being crushed by Kim Il-Sung's concentration of personal power appeared even before the Korean War (1950–1953), as his image already was paraded in mass gatherings and stamped onto the headings of newspapers in the late 1940s. The Korean War could have led to Kim's downfall, given that North Korea came close to defeat after four months, but he was saved by China's entrance into the war on the North's behalf in late October 1950.

In the mid-1950s, Kim ramped up the killing of his potential rivals, whether they were Korean–Soviet advisors, leftists with Chinese ties like Gim Won-bong, or native Korean communist leaders like Bak Heon-yeong. When such more ideologically sound, former independence activists grew alarmed at Kim Il-Sung's monopolization of authority, they had appealed to the Soviet Union and China to intervene. They tried, but just at this time a major rift between these communist powers also emerged, and Kim played the two off each other in order to save himself. This moment, from 1956 to 1957, was perhaps the last realistic chance to turn away from what North Korea eventually became. Thereafter, the rationale for North Korea's ruling system, indeed for the country itself, became firmly tied to maintaining the absolute supremacy of one man, which made the later hereditary succession almost inevitable.

It was not just political rivals who fell victim to this totalitarian descent beginning in the 1950s. Skilled and well-intentioned writers, artists, academics, professionals and others found themselves trapped in a country regimented to service the Kim regime. Many of them simply "disappeared," not only by losing their jobs or lives but also by becoming erased from history. Like the purged political figures, these educated Koreans would have been the leaders of an alternative North Korea that never came to be.

Thankfully many of them, whose works and accomplishments were banned in South Korea during the South's own dictatorship era, eventually won recognition in the South following democratization, but this also demonstrates that

North Korea's reason for being was always fundamentally connected to that of the South. North Korean history, including the two dynastic successions of 1994 and 2011, developed consistently in opposition to South Korea, whose own character and orientation underwent dramatic transformations. South Korea's historical transitions offered a steady reminder of North Korea's original possibilities, but they also had the effect of further closing alternative paths to North Korea's historical development until they precluded any valid reason for its existence at all.

Chapter 73

ORIGINS OF KOREA'S POLITICAL CORRUPTION

Every major election season in South Korea seems to bring forth a scramble among politicians to break away from, rearrange, and construct new alliances. This cycle of party formation and destruction has characterized South Korean politics since liberation from Japanese colonial rule in 1945.

What seems to get lost in all this is the idea of public service, that holding elected office is a duty, not a prize or instrument for personal gain. With government office comes the great responsibility to use political authority not for oneself, but for the greater good. Notwithstanding the chronic failure to live up to them, such ideals have been around for a very long time. They lay at the heart of Confucian political teachings that entered Korea more than a thousand years ago and drove political development thereafter.

So why has it been so difficult to realize these ideals in Korean political culture? Why do many South Korean political and government officials remain so prone to treating their offices as vehicles for self-aggrandizement or, even worse, as money-making ventures? In short, why is corruption still such a problem?

Despite over three decades as an electoral democracy and an even longer history of press monitoring of politics, South Korea still consistently ranks embarrassingly low in the periodic surveys of corruption around the world. Habits of paying people in power, from policemen to presidents, to gain access, attention and outcomes seem ingrained among South Koreans, as if they were born with this inclination. This cannot be true, of course, any more than it is for people living in other countries suffering from chronic corruption. And there seems no definitive answer to explain this behavior, aside from turning to Korean history to find possible origins.

We can begin with Confucianism itself, which values not only hierarchy in social relations but also reciprocity, the idea that one should repay kind treatment. This is in general a good thing, but in the political arena, as reformers observed hundreds of years ago, this can lead to officials expecting something in return for their decisions. And just as powerfully, it triggers the impulse to pay bribes, even irrespective of the official's wishes, knowing that the official will feel obligated to return the favor. Confucian political culture also worked together with deeply rooted forms of social hierarchy in Korea, which ordered people according to their birth identity (the social standing of their parents and ancestors), to turn government office into the most desired and prestigious occupation. Political or bureaucratic office, in sum, became the object and reflection of status (and power) more than a means of public service, although such behavior actually contradicted Confucian ideals, as Korean critics repeatedly noted in the past.

In the Joseon era, another product of this complex, distinctive mixture of Confucian ideals and hereditary social organization were the *hyangni* (more commonly known as "ajeon"). These clerks, bound by birth as if they were enslaved into this position (which was not untrue), ran the day-to-day operations of local governments. As they had to be, they were administrative experts, managing tax assessment and collection, policing, and a wide range of other functions that their social superiors, the hereditary aristocracy ("yangban"), simply were unprepared to do. But for all this, the *hyangni* clerks were not even regularly paid; they were expected to "skim off the top" while collecting the taxes. Despite the regular outcries over these clerks' venality (what a surprise), the Joseon dynasty did little to abolish or even reform this system of legalized corruption.

That the descendants of these hereditary clerks, during the transition to the modern era, went on to take commanding positions among the new social elite as landlords, politicians and businessmen probably has something to do with the persistence of corruption. This is an educated guess, however--almost impossible to prove--although it is not difficult to find *hyangni* ancestry among local notables around the country even now.

Despite all of these deeply embedded sources of the culture of political corruption, what appears as likely the single biggest cause—so big, in fact, that it might dwarf the others—is Korea's long and strong history of authoritarianism. Of course, Korea had always had a dictatorship, strictly speaking, and autocratic Japanese colonial rulers in the early twentieth century would hardly have prioritized public service for the sake of Koreans. But from 1948 to 1987, for the most part, South Korea was ruled by a succession of native dictatorships, which deployed all the modern mechanisms of domination, surveillance and mobilization. Dictatorships by definition lack accountability and transparency, and hence they operate substantially through informal means— what we easily recognize as corruption—regardless of formal laws. This is particularly true for one-party dictatorships, but one-man dictatorship, which is what South Korea usually got, can be just as lethal to developing an honest and responsive political system.

So while things have gotten a lot better since democratization, as shown in the 2016–2017 candlelight demonstrations and prosecutions that brought down President Park Geun-hye, the political realm (together with business) still appears to be struggling to meet the clearly broad yearning for fairness and accountability, a fervent sentiment actually in place even during the dictatorships. It was, after all, what brought democracy to the country in the first place.

Chapter 74

ANTI-COMMUNISM'S
POWERFUL HOLD

When the Obama administration of the United States moved to normalize relations with Cuba in 2015, a minor uproar arose in protest, the most fervent of which came from the older members of the Cuban exile community in Florida who had fled the island nation after the communist takeover in the late 1950s. This community, however, remains relatively small, and their views on communism seem increasingly simplistic and outdated.

Now multiply the effects of such sentiments tenfold, and you have South Korea, or more specifically the older generation of South Koreans who still see communism as among the greatest threats and evils. Like the Cubans in South Florida, these South Koreans are the product of their country's long struggle against a communist state, and so it is understandable that they hold such views. But these views are just as antiquated as those of the Florida Cubans, and sadly, they continue to hold some sway over South Korea today. Why?

To answer, we must begin by recognizing the historical roots of this rabid anti-communism, which played a central role in the birth of South Korea itself in the late 1940s. Immediately following the end of World War II and Korea's liberation from Japanese colonial rule in 1945, anti-communism was implanted and enforced by the American occupation, and then used as a tool for repression, mobilization and legitimization by successive South Korean dictatorships. Within half a year after the establishment of the Republic of Korea in 1948, the government headed by President Syngman Rhee instituted the National Security Law as an all-inclusive legal mechanism to stifle political opposition.

Since then, this law, born and developed in parallel with South Korea itself, has outlasted five different constitutional systems and an enormous degree of social, economic and cultural change. Throughout South Korea's history, the National Security Law acted as the symbol, originator and enforcer of the fear of communism, thus serving the interests of various dictatorships in legitimatizing their rule and in suppressing resistance.

The most egregious application of this and other anti-communist statutes came in 1975 when the "Yushin" dictatorship under Park Chung-Hee arrested scores of dissidents with fabricated charges of communist activities. It then staged a kangaroo court that sentenced to death eight of these inno-cent people, who were quickly executed within a day. The Supreme Court, which upheld this ruling, will always be stained by this shameful act. But the legal tool used to support such outrageous action remained, and it continued to legitimize arbitrary arrests and prosecutions, as well as torture and state killings. In fact, the National Security Law still states today that violations can be punishable by execution.

Such was the power and politics of anti-communism, indeed to an extent that younger South Koreans today would find unimaginable. But at the height of the Yushin dictatorship, students began to examine more closely the circumstances of the superpower occupation, national division, and autocracy that had given birth to the South Korean state in the 1940s and 1950s. What they found was that communism was a much more complicated topic than what they had been taught and what most people took for granted. Many South Koreans, as they were told, had simply equated communism with North Korea, without wondering how communism or socialism arose around the world, or why it might have been so appealing to Koreans in the earlier part of the twentieth century.

Sadly, many of these South Koreans, mostly now in their 60s and older, are mired in their former experience of indoctrination under dictatorship and still react almost instinctively by blurting out "commie" (*ppalgaengi*) or simply "leftist." Remarkably, there might be just as many South Korean adherents to anti-communism as North Korean believers of communism, given its absurd distortions by the Northern regime. In South Korean politics, it remains at times profitable to engage in red-baiting, or implying that political opponents are communist, and to stoke the fear of communism by using North Korea as a convenient excuse.

A case in point is the National Security Law itself: After declining in use significantly, beginning with the presidency of Lee Myung-bak in 2008 the application of the law for all kinds of prosecutorial actions grew precipitously. Although the law's opening clause was amended after democratization to emphasize "threats against the liberal democratic order," it still forbids not only actions, but even the expression of thoughts, in speech or writing, that can be construed as "anti-state."

One does not even have to approve of North Korea's government or ideology; simply saying something positive about its people or society can warrant arrest. The bald contradiction between, on the one hand, the legalized suppression of free speech, and on the other, the claims of protecting a "liberal democratic order," seems tragically not to matter much. The ingrained fear of North Korea's ideological influence, however ridiculous this seems in this day and age, persists. Despite democratization, then, South Koreans, especially the elderly, remain beholden to their history, in an almost juvenile manner. Perhaps a truer maturation of this society can emerge only with the passing of its most mature generations.

Chapter 75

FRAUDULENT CAPTAINS OF THE SEWOL FERRY DISASTER

Mid-April has now become a time to pause and reflect on the saddest event in South Korea in a generation, the sinking of the Sewol ferry on April 16, 2014: what happened, why it happened, and the meaning of it all for the country's identity and future. For like all such defining historical moments, the impact of this disaster extends far into both the future and the past. Not only did the country forever change with the harrowing deaths of over 300 very innocent lives, but the way one looks back at South Korea's history has followed suit. In remembering this awful event, then, let us reconsider its significance in a broader historical framework.

First of all, investigations into the tragedy have revealed that this was not an "accident" but almost an inevitability, an accident waiting to happen. The many direct factors, both large and small, all resulted from choices made by actors in the government, the shipping industry, and the ferry company to violate laws, regulations and common decency. These actions in turn were driven by a larger culture of greed, abuse, negligence, and the blind pursuit of individual interests over that of the community. In moments of painful reflection, however, South Koreans came to realize that these more indirect factors implicated their society as a whole, which raised troubling issues about their collective identity and history.

What, then, were the origins and turning points of the larger context that converged on that fateful day? What were, in sum, the structural causes of this tragedy? This is the question that historians will be asking ten, twenty and fifty years from now. But we can anticipate some of those findings already.

Despite the reprehensible, unfathomable actions of the ship's captain that day, the decisions that led to putting hundreds of lives in the hands of such an unqualified person were just as unforgivable. This leads us to the ferry company's owners and managers, but also to the bureaucrats who failed to enforce safety rules regarding personnel, the seaworthiness of the ship, and the amount of cargo it could carry. Such were the ingredients to a toxic brew of incompetence, sloth and corruption. But as South Korea's history has repeatedly made clear, the close relationship between the government and the "captains" of industry shaped a culture of indulgence and misbehavior on both sides, even in regards to public safety. The headlong rush toward industrialization and economic development produced an extraordinary increase in the quality of material life and lifted millions of South Koreans out of poverty, but the costs were equally stunning, including the prioritization of speed and results over propriety and process.

Still, after more than a quarter century since democratization in South Korea, the Sewol passengers and their families had to assume that the system of checks and oversight, or at least the institutional mechanisms to respond to such an event, were functioning. It turned out otherwise. The coast guard had no meaningful rescue plan for such an incident and did not know what to do, and shockingly, neither did the emergency response agencies of the local or central government. This remarkable sense of confusion inflicted the entire chain of command, all the way to the Blue House, where President Park Geun-hye seemed uninformed and paralyzed that day.

We may never know why the highest levels of government could do so little in those crucial first hours when the chances of saving the passengers were the highest. But we can ask how, like the ferry captain and the corrupt officials, someone who was not ready for the job could have been placed in position as the "captain" of the country. In 2012, a slim majority of the South Korean electorate chose as the president someone whose primary claim to qualification was being the child of a former dictator. Many of these voters were surely motivated by a more complex mix of considerations, including ideology, but for others, this family connection was enough, as if this were North, not South, Korea. If we dig a little deeper, we must question how this person could have been poised, twice no less, to become the conservative party's presidential nominee. And here we find that, despite democratization, South Korea continued to be run largely by an autocratic style of personality-based politics.

Cynical hangers-on and manipulating enablers in the political realm chose to exploit the popular nostalgia for the developmentalist, authoritarian past over building a stronger democracy. Ideally, in a democratic society, the people are responsible not only for choosing their leaders, but for preserving the viability of their democracy with a culture of fairness, transparency and accountability. This includes the careful consideration of the major forces, especially from their collective past, that have shaped the people's outlook and behavior. As South Korean citizens attempt to draw lessons from this tragedy, they must undertake such a frank examination of their history, and then work to overcome it. That would be the best way to honor the victims and bring comfort to their suffering families.

Chapter 76

OVERCOMING PAST HIERARCHIES

As someone whose profession depends on the spread of knowledge and understanding, I rarely advocate the suppression of information. Still, one cannot but feel somewhat uneasy with the periodic "outings" of pro-Japanese figures from Korea's colonial period (1910–1945), because such exercises seem to have a punitive quality to them.

On the one hand, there is much value to shining a light on the ways Koreans collaborated with the Japanese occupation regime. As these campaigns allege, collaborators often took advantage of, or otherwise benefited from, the severely discriminatory means of foreign rule, and as a matter of historical record they should be known.

On the other hand, these "collaborators" mostly did not participate in the excesses of the colonial regime, much of which took place over the colonial period's closing half-decade, when Koreans were mobilized for the Pacific War. The majority of these "pro-Japanese" Koreans did not kidnap, coerce, or trick their compatriots into forced labor or the "comfort stations" of sexual slavery, for example, or torture political prisoners, or work to destroy Korean nationhood in order to enforce loyalty to Japan.

Most Korean government officials, businessmen, and others who benefited from or even joined the colonial system simply tried to do the best they could for themselves and their families. That they failed to actively resist Japanese rule does not necessarily mean that they committed treason, or any crime for that matter.

The problem with this more sympathetic view, however, is that the unjust hierarchies of the colonial regime remained, in many ways, the basis for the inequalities of South Korean society, indeed all the way to the present day. The descendants of those who benefited from colonial rule built upon their inherited privileges, often by colluding with the structures of severe exploitation and discrimination in the succeeding South Korean dictatorships. And now, these people's descendants, who remain largely ignorant of or disregard this painful history of unjust inequalities, not only occupy political and social positions of power but fight against efforts to bring about greater fairness in society.

And not surprisingly, many of them also insist on covering up or distorting the more uncomfortable aspects of their nation's history. They like to believe that somehow their privileged standing today resulted from only their forebears' hard work or other legitimate gains. To use a baseball analogy from the United States, it is as if they think they hit a home run when actually they were born on third base.

What is taking place in the United States can in fact be illuminating. In some ways, the racial imbalance today might be stronger than ever, despite the gains made by African Americans economically. This is because they are disproportionately victimized by the country's discriminatory criminal justice system, which compounds the socioeconomic inequalities into a perpetual cycle of hardship. While most white Americans understand that today's racial inequality is rooted in America's horrible past of slavery, most of them cannot recognize that their own privileges depend on the continuation of that past. The majority of white Americans, in other words, cannot see that, despite the end of slavery 150 years ago or even the end of legal discrimination half a century ago, there can never be a "clean slate" from which American society could restart. Indeed, such ignorance is itself a form of discrimination, and this explains today's intractable racial gaps in privileges and economic standing.

In South Korea, then, great progress can be made in overcoming the constant politicization of the nation's history if those who are privileged can recognize that, first, they are indeed privileged, and not necessarily entitled to their position. Second, the privileged can honestly acknowledge that their parents or relatives might have benefited from collusion with the past structures of unjust inequality, such as colonial rule or the South Korean dictatorships, and that the advantages from one period built upon the advantages of a preceding one. And third, everyone, not just the privileged, can benefit from viewing collaboration with the South Korean dictatorships on equal terms with collaboration with Japanese colonial rule. Unjust inequality from exploitation is precisely that, regardless of whether the authoritarian ruling systems were led by Japanese or Koreans.

This would also make it easier for forgiveness to work its magic. People should not be blamed for what their forebears might have done, but they must first acknowledge what their forebears probably did. An alternative would be to confiscate the material benefits or political rights of those in privileged positions today. This is what happens in social revolutions, and I do not think South Koreans can risk the likely terrible upheavals of such a step. But such unhealthy historical ignorance and disregard also cannot continue without risking an even further sharpening of the political and social divides.

Chapter 77

GRIPPED BY THE AUTHORITARIAN MINDSET

The so-called Taegukgi rallies of 2016 and 2017 in favor of President Park Geun-hye were telling in several ways, including the appearance, amid the sea of South Korean flags (Taegukgi), of American flags. Although the Stars and Stripes have appeared often in conservative protests over the years, it was usually to commemorate the Korean War or in support of .the United States in some way. The American flag's unfurling in rallies that fiercely opposed Park Geun-hye's impeachment seemed more difficult to fathom.

Another interesting feature of these protests was that almost all of the protestors had black hair, although more close-up photos of their faces confirmed that these demonstrators overwhelmingly were senior citizens. This seems highly symbolic: As if to deny that time has indeed passed, these determined marchers were somewhat stuck in the past, and not only by keeping up their hair-dyeing routines. Whether one hears them in news interviews or speaks to them personally, one cannot help feeling that they are gripped by a fixed view from the days of authoritarianism and colonization.

Colonization here refers not only to the period of Japanese rule, from 1910 to 1945, but also to the domination of the United States in South Korea in the decades after liberation. In this system, America served as a model of advancement and source of aid, but also as a global patron of South Korea's developmentalist dictatorship. To these elderly citizens today, the United States stands first and foremost as the nation's savior in the Korean War, when the American-led UN forces helped South Korea escape conquest by the communists. Thereafter in the 1960s, when the United States requested military support from President Park Chung-Hee's government for the Vietnam War, tens of thousands of South Korean troops were sent to Southeast Asia.

To probably the majority from this period, such formative experiences cemented the bond between the United States, anti-communism, South Korea's economic growth out of poverty, and Park Chung-Hee. Park had integrated these components into his program for modernization and to

Figure 77.1 Commemorative photo of President Park Chung Hee at the 1970 groundbreaking ceremony of Pohang Ironworks, POSCO Museum, Pohang, South Korea.

legitimate his rule, which in the 1970s turned iron fisted to keep the people in line in the name of industrialization and the struggle against North Korea.

This explains why many elderly Koreans attached themselves to Park's daughter when she reentered national politics in the late 1990s. To them, no amount of evidence to the contrary could shake their faith in Park Geun-hye's inherent goodness, based on their image of her father and their frozen perspective about what was ultimately at stake: no less than the fate of the country that they, the true patriots, built with their hard work and sacrifice.

The frenzy with which some of these Taegukgi demonstrators, in 2016–2017, applied their colonized worldview further testified to the continuing hold of the authoritarian past, when the threat of physical force and blind subservience to a strong leader seemed the norm. Such behavior included the shockingly prominent display, along with the South Korean and American flags, of signs in these rallies that read, "Martial law is the only solution," or "If it's commies, killing them is fine," in reference to their political opponents. The readiness to turn to heavy-handed, violent methods, straight from the dictatorship period, also appeared in the menacing protests, with even weapons in hand, in front of the homes of constitutional court justices and of the independent prosecutor investigating the Park scandal.

It was as if the political liberalization and democratization over the preceding three decades, when the rule of law and peaceful tolerance for opposition were supposed to have increased, had never happened. Or more accurately, it was as if the changes were too fast and jarring for mindsets that had been powerfully molded by the country's turbulent past, during which lives were shaped by more immediate concerns of survival amid foreign intervention, war, poverty, and other forms of unrest.

This is why, as much as we need to rebuke those who employed violence and intimidation in the Taegukgi rallies, I am also inclined to view these South Koreans with sympathy. They, too, are victims of the past, even if they see themselves as victims of the present.

Chapter 78

WAYS OF LIVING HISTORY

Having to experience most of the extraordinary events of 2016 in South Korea remotely, I was grateful for the internet's powers of live transmission, but I still felt that I was missing out on history as it was being made. For the millions of South Koreans coming out to the streets on those fall Saturdays, there was an unmistakably stirring, even a festive, sense of living history, that their collective action was determining the fate of the nation itself.

Among the extraordinary outcomes of the candlelight demonstrations and the removal of President Park Geun-hye from office was that the process blew open the lid of the country's modern history. This result, then, stood as another dimension of living history: Because of the personal and institutional connections that directly extended to the military dictatorship period of the 1970s and 1980s, we eventually were compelled to think and uncover as much about the past as the present. And in the aftermath, we came to better understand what core people and patterns from South Korea's authoritarian period survived, and what behaviors, customs and connections continued to exert influence despite the formal political liberalization over the preceding three decades. For surely these revelations carried a strong historical bent and cast a dark shadow over the lineages of economic and political power that reached back to the days of autocracy. Here, then, are some sketches of the revised picture of the recent past that emerged:

First, the Yushin dictatorship of the 1970s under the command of Park Chung-Hee, the ousted president's father, depended far more on corruption than has been generally understood. There is a treasured impression among many South Koreans still today that while Park Chung-Hee led an authoritarian system, he and his regime were not corrupt. This of course defies logic, but the glorification of rapid economic development has obscured the networks of bribery, extortion, and coercion that were central to the dictatorship and, as is now clear, never went away.

Access to Park Chung-Hee, not surprisingly, remained in the hands of a few people, including his personal bodyguard, the Korean Central Intelligence Agency (KCIA) director (who eventually assassinated Park and his bodyguard), and Park's daughter Geun-hye. And those figures, in turn, could exercise and remain open to the thriving impulses of influence-peddling cultivated by the close relationship between Park's government and big business since the 1960s. But influence over his daughter, it appears, was enough for even smaller fry to quickly gain wealth and power, despite the concerns raised by the KCIA and other government agencies.

Second, we know of religion's major role in the political and cultural development of the 1970s, particularly the impact of the Catholic church and of some other religious leaders in the opposition movement, and we know generally that most Protestants were pro-regime, driven by their anti-communism. But the stunning effect of Choe Tae-min, the church figure who came to hold such sway over Park Geun-hye after her mother's death in 1974, raises troubling questions about the extent to which the Protestant establishment as a whole was embedded in the authoritarian system, and how much this relationship continued to affect political affairs thereafter.

This leads us to the durability of Park Chung-Hee's personality cult, including the ways it hid the real behavior and family circumstances of the man. Over time, uncomfortable details were revealed from credible eyewitnesses of the 1960s and 1970s. No need to enumerate them here, but let's just say that it would have been surprising if Park Geun-hye had emerged from these conditions with something resembling sound judgment. In any case, the interaction of political, economic and religious factors with her status as the strongman's daughter compels more careful consideration of the forces, building on that original personality cult, that eventually enabled her to become elected as president of a democratic South Korea.

The precise balance between such structural factors and individual actions is always difficult to pin down, and none of these discoveries will likely absolve Park Geun-hye herself, but she was undoubtedly also a victim of her personal history as well as that of the country. And while this shockingly distasteful connection between her and the Choe family fueled wild speculation and absurd rumors, as well as a lot of ridicule thanks to the plentiful hints of sex and intrigue, it was mostly a sad, distressing story.

But a redeeming feature of this scandalous and trying episode was that, in the end, it brought about disclosures that highlighted yet another facet of living history: that the present determines to a great extent the past, which is the opposite of the logic of history that we are accustomed to. It also showed again that the purpose of studying history is to learn about the past in order to overcome it instead of being bound by it. That's what makes living history worthwhile.

INDEX